MY WHIRLWIND LIVES
NAVIGATING DECADES OF STORMS

A POLITICAL MEMOIR ... & MANIFESTO

GUERNICA WORLD EDITIONS 51

DEE KNIGHT

MY WHIRLWIND LIVES

NAVIGATING DECADES OF STORMS

GUERNICA
World
EDITIONS

TORONTO—CHICAGO—BUFFALO—LANCASTER (U.K.)

2022

Michael Mirolla, general editor
Interior design: Dee Knight
Cover design: Lisa Amowitz

Guernica Editions Inc.
287 Templemead Drive, Hamilton (ON), Canada L8W 2W4
2250 Military Road, Tonawanda, N.Y. 14150-6000 U.S.A.
www.guernicaeditions.com

Distributors:
Independent Publishers Group (IPG)
600 North Pulaski Road, Chicago IL 60624
University of Toronto Press Distribution (UTP)
5201 Dufferin Street, Toronto (ON), Canada M3H 5T8
Gazelle Book Services, White Cross Mills
High Town, Lancaster LA1 4XS U.K.

First edition.

Legal Deposit—First Quarter
Library of Congress Catalog Card Number: 2021949674

Library and Archives Canada Cataloguing in Publication
Title: My whirlwind lives / Dee Knight. Names: Knight, Dee, author.
Series: Guernica world editions; 51. Description: 1st edition. | Series
statement: Guernica world editions; 51 Identifiers: Canadiana (print)
20210353864 | Canadiana (ebook) 20210353899 | ISBN 9781771837200
(softcover) | ISBN 9781771837248 (EPUB) Subjects: LCSH: Knight, Dee. |
LCSH: Social reformers—United States—Biography. | LCSH: Political
activists—United States—Biography. | LCGFT: Autobiographies.
Classification: LCC HN65 .K65 2022 | DDC 303.48/4092—dc23

About Dee Knight's Memoir:

My Whirlwind Lives *is a fast-paced and fascinating tour of a life filled with politics, passion and purpose. Knight takes us through decades of turmoil in the U.S. and overseas, and decades of movement building against war, injustice and destruction of the planet.*

The book is infused with Knight's sweeping vision of a more humane world and his infectious sense of optimism. Read it and act.

— **Medea Benjamin**, *Co-founder, CodePink (*<u>codepink.org</u>*)*

Table of Contents

IMAGE CREDITS:

Dedication

This book is dedicated to the Movement for Black Lives,
whose courage ignited the beginning of genuine change;
to About Face/Veterans Against the War,
and to the families of all these veterans,
whose lives were significantly damaged,
and often cut tragically short, by the U.S. war machine.
And also to all active-duty U.S. GIs, that they will know
they have wholehearted support as they learn the truth.

And to the new generation that is deciding to take over.

Acknowledgements

This book is a response to current stormy events and trends that are changing history. But it's a special response, looking not just at recent experiences, but viewing them through a prism of five decades of resistance and *real* protest. There is a list of people who helped form my understanding of these events. Alexandria Ocasio-Cortez (AOC) and Bernie Sanders are among the most recent, along with the rest of the growing "squad" – Jamaal Bowman (my friend and local rep), Rashida Tlaib, Ilhan Omar, Ayanna Pressley and Cori Bush.

The friends and mentors who shared my experience living in exile in Canada during the Vietnam war from 1968–74, included Stan Pietlock, who launched Amex-Canada as the newsletter of the Union of American Exiles in 1968; Charles and Maryanne Campbell; Jack Colhoun, who made me aware of the importance of struggling for amnesty; Gerry Condon, Sandy Rutherford, Steve Grossman and Evangeline Mix Lantana, who were key members of the Amex leadership group. Amex close friend Joe Jones corrected this manuscript.

Terry Klug, Andy Stapp, and John Catalinotto – organizers and leaders of the American Servicemen's Union (ASU), helped reshape my understanding of the GI resistance, and became my long-time friends and comrades. John Catalinotto's recent book about the ASU, *Turn the Guns Around,* has also been an important inspiration. Another major influence was the late Gabriel Kolko, author of *The Roots of American Foreign Policy* and other important books.

Nicaragua's Sandinista Front for National Liberation provided me with a unique opportunity to witness and help a dynamic revolution, which continues. Portugal's movement for *Poder Popular* (people power) showed me that revolution is possible in an advanced European country, even if it's faced with major challenges.

The bold new vision led by Alexandria Ocasio-Cortez, and the hard-slogging socialist organizing of the Democratic Socialists of America (DSA), have opened real possibilities for a Green New Deal.

Many people, in addition to those named here, have influenced my political growth and understanding during the past five decades. I take full responsibility for my mistakes and omissions, and thank all of these people for their help and patience along the way.

Introduction:

The Whirlwind Begins

The storm we've witnessed recently didn't start in 2020, or 2016. It started decades ago, in the 1960s.

You could feel the storm brewing. Something was "blowin' in the wind." But it was a whirlwind: threats of nuclear catastrophe over Cuba blaring on the TV news, then police dogs and rednecks terrorizing civil rights marchers down south, then Vietnamese children fleeing from napalm flames. Then draft notices to go to Vietnam to "fight commies."

I only heard Dylan's "The Times They Are A-Changin'" vaguely at first. I was a small-town boy from eastern Oregon. In my high school "modern problems" class in 1964, I voted in a straw poll for the right-winger Goldwater against the "peace candidate" Johnson. Together with his running mate, "Bombs Away" Curtis LeMay, Goldwater proposed nuking Vietnam "back to the stone age." Ronald Reagan and George H.W. Bush both were Goldwater's friends and strong supporters. Lyndon Johnson defeated Goldwater in 1964, running as a "peace candidate."

The next year, at college in San Francisco, word spread that LBJ was sending half a million troops to Vietnam. I heard friends talk of conscientious objection, or refusing the draft. Some asked me what I planned to do. I couldn't answer. I didn't know. There were also reports in the school paper of students going south to join "freedom riders" in Mississippi to help with voter registration.

The quadrangle on the San Francisco State College campus buzzed every day with learning opportunities. Anti-war students organized "teach-ins" on the war. The Black Students Union had speakers there nearly every day. They said the draft was based on class and race privilege. Working class boys, especially Black ones, got drafted while middle class boys, especially white ones, got student deferments. They said the whole war was racist.

One friend was applying for conscientious objector status. Another was already planning to head for Canada. The Spring 1967 Mobilization Against the War marched past my apartment complex facing the Golden Gate Park panhandle in San Francisco. As I sat watching from the low-slung fence in front of my apartment building which faced the park, a classmate waved and beckoned me to join. That's all it took, after all I had been learning. I literally jumped off the fence and began marching. It was my first anti-war protest –

one of many. Not long after that I was collecting signatures on campus by the dozens for the newly formed Peace and Freedom Party. PFP has been on the ballot ever since.

I felt my life changing fast. When I jumped off the fence and joined the protest, I made a decision. By the fall I submitted an application for conscientious objector (CO) status. It was my first act of war resistance. My small town draft board told me they wouldn't consider it while I had a student deferment. What happened next was bizarre: I saw an ad in *The Progressive* magazine to join the anti-war presidential campaign of Eugene McCarthy in Wisconsin. The appeal caught me: "you can help stop the war. Come to Wisconsin. Help Eugene McCarthy beat Johnson." It got me. I decided to abandon my student deferment, sell my books and fly there.

When I phoned home from Madison, Wisconsin, in January 1968 to tell my parents I had left college to try and end the war, my mother said she hoped I would not get in trouble with the government. I told her the government had already gotten in trouble with *me*. In August 1968, I participated in the "battle of Chicago" at the Democratic National Convention – not as a "front liner," really more of an observer. The cops' message was clear: standing against the war would get your head beat.

After the Chicago mayhem I caught a ride to Toronto, Canada – aware it would take a long time to stop the war machine. I wrote home to tell my parents I was in Canada. Four years later I wrote again, to say charges against me for refusing the draft had been dismissed on a technicality. I returned to the U.S. briefly that year, to build support for a true amnesty for war resisters of all kinds. Then I went back to Canada, to continue working with Amex-Canada, the American exile/expatriate war resister group and magazine that led the amnesty movement from 1972-77.

All this was a prelude for me. During the most intense anti-war protests, from 1969 to '71, I was out of the country. But after the draft refusal charges against me were dismissed in early 1972, I became a leader of the fight for amnesty. It was a years-long slog, with intensive organizing among exiled war resisters in Canada, Sweden, France and England; alliance development with anti-war Vietnam veterans; constant media work, as well as national speaking tours and meetings to develop a winning coalition for amnesty. There were some "magic moments," like the live national TV nomination of a war resister for vice president at the 1976 Democratic National Convention, and "surfacing" military resister Gerry Condon at a Washington, DC conference despite the fact he had been court-martialed and carried a ten-year prison sentence. Over those years we won much of what we had demanded, and the experiences of that time helped shape my commitment to change.

Visiting countries where revolutions were actually happening – Portugal during the "Carnation Revolution" of 1974-75, and Sandinista Nicaragua during the 1980s – gave me insight into real revolutions, and the fact that the U.S. government would always put them down, whatever it took.

Now there's the battle for a Green New Deal to save the planet; In 2020 street protests raged in cities across the country and the world, to say Black Lives Matter. The official U.S. response to the coronavirus pandemic caused hundreds of thousands of deaths, and brought on the worst depression since the 1930s.

What's the connection among all these things? They're all part of reclaiming a peaceful, just and sustainable planet, and our lives.

I jumped into the whirlwind more than 50 years ago, hoping and expecting change to come quickly and easily. Now I know better. But the change is coming. There's a hurricane outside. It's early to say how long it will last, or what it will bring. My hope is it will stimulate us not merely to save the planet but to help the people of the USA and the world escape from capitalist never-never land, and bring about a world we can believe in.

Reflection:

Some of the events I tell about could be considered sad. I tend not to write about sadness. I think it's partly due to my father's influence. He was a naturally cheerful person, despite being dead serious about everything. One of his favorite cheerful expressions, which he would say occasionally to my mom, was "ain't it grand?" Both his sisters also said this from time to time. I think it had a quasi-religious basis – accepting whatever the lord chose to give.

None of this meant sadness didn't exist or wasn't acceptable. It just wasn't expressed. There was a determination to *deal with* or *cope with* or *fix* whatever. It signaled a "can do" attitude. After bringing seven children into the world as a saddle maker, my dad finally decided the only way we could have the house my mom wanted was to make it from scratch. So that's what he did. He found and bought a lot in the riverside suburb of the eastern Oregon town we lived in, and proceeded to build a house. It took three years. While he was building, he moved our family to a former army barracks near the airport on the opposite side of town. We joked that it was well insulated, because snow stayed on at least part of the house during most of the winter. On the heated half the snow melted away.

After my dad finished the house we couldn't afford to live in it. So we rented a big old house in the downtown area, behind the newspaper plant, half a block from the river. My dad also got a new job. Instead of making saddles, which he loved, he sold life insurance, which he didn't love as much. But he was good at it. He told me once it doesn't matter what you do, as long as you're the best at it.

It took another three years before we could afford to live in the house my dad built. It was designed as my mom wanted, with the kitchen and dining area looking out over the large living room, with five bedrooms, three bathrooms and a utility room. A family of nine, plus Grandma, could fit in it. The back yard was big enough for a generous vegetable garden plus a modest lawn. My dad's favorite activity was working in the garden, which first involved removing all the rocks from the former riverbed. His sons were encouraged to help with that. We also helped Mom can vegetables we picked from trees about an hour's drive from our new home. And we rode our bicycles into town to our part-time jobs which helped pay for Catholic school. It was all good fun, and we were never really sad.

1 – Fake News and Fake Protests

The former president talked a lot about "fake news." As if we needed examples, he whipped up a flurry of claims of vote fraud, which he said stole his landslide 2020 electoral victory. To make it all appear real, he mobilized supporters from across the country to go to Washington to "stop the steal," and thus prove the official reports of his defeat were fake.

The resulting mob assault on the capitol was not really a protest. It was a fake insurrection – a pretense of an attempted coup, without military or other substantial support. Even the soon-to-be-former president disclaimed it as it fizzled, after it caused five deaths.

It's important to distinguish between fake protests and real ones, and between real revolutions and their opposite. Popular protests involve large numbers of people, oppressed or outraged by unjust government actions or policies, mobilizing to stop the injustice. The mob assault on the capital was more of a group *tantrum,* an act of revenge egged on by a disappointed would-be dictator. It was also a threat, aimed at stopping a change to their cherished *status quo.* The mobsters were fascinated at their break-in, thrilled they could scare some elected officials. And then they left.

I felt both irony and revulsion watching the rightwing mob storm the U.S. capitol on January 6, 2020. Witnessing mild police resistance to white gun-toting rioters rushing the capitol behind the Confederate flag reminded me in contrast of earlier scenes. I recalled the summer night six months earlier, when police and soldiers used tear gas and other weapons against real Black Lives Matter protesters to clear a path for the president to walk with his entourage across the street to a church, brandishing a bible.

The scene took me back to earlier confrontations in Washington. In October 1967 tens of thousands of anti-war protesters stormed the Pentagon, armed with flowers, determined to force peace on the war makers. At the August 1963 March on Washington, a quarter million people, mainly African Americans from the South, joined Martin Luther King, Jr., demanding jobs and freedom. They heard King's "I Have a Dream" speech. King said "In a sense we've come to our nation's capital to cash a check. When the architects of our republic wrote the magnificent words of the Constitution and the Declaration of Independence, they were signing a promissory note to which every American was to fall heir. This note was a promise that all men, yes, Black men as well as white men, would be guaranteed the inalienable rights of life, liberty, and the pursuit of happiness."

In a sense we're still trying to cash that check. Not the down payment in the form of extended unemployment benefits during the pandemic, or the bailout for struggling corner stores, restaurants, or gig businesses. The check MLK mentioned is different. It's what Georgia voters redeemed in November 2020 and again in January 2021 – fulfillment of the promise of basic rights, including the right to vote. The fact that they got it infuriated Trump so much that he called on his supporters to storm the capitol hoping to force Congress to call it fraud.

For a century after the end of the U.S. Civil War, the mere act of voting was a crime for Black people, punishable by death without trial. It took endless organizing and marching in the 1950s and early 1960s to begin to change that. Those were real protests. The fake protest on January 6 was a threat to return to the Jim Crow era.

Assembling in Washington to demand rights and redress is different from storming the capitol to stop the process of validating votes. These things can be confusing. Some background might help.

I went to Washington on July 4, 1974, to demand, together with Vietnam Veterans Against the War, that Richard Nixon resign. He left office a month later, in the face of an impeachment that was sure to convict him. When Vice President Gerald Ford took over, the first thing he did was pardon Nixon. Ford then proposed a "clemency program" for war resisters (official and unofficial conscientious objectors). From Toronto, we (the exiled war resisters) perceived it as cover for pardoning Nixon, and unjustly punitive since it stipulated two years of "alternative service." So we organized a successful boycott of the program.

Ford lasted just to the end of Nixon's term, when Jimmy Carter was elected, promising change. My fellow war resisters and I had a hand in that change: his first act as president was amnesty – a full pardon for *some* war resisters. We had pressed for this at the 1976 Democratic Party convention in New York. I had returned from Canada to organize and fight for this change, which was a victory for our efforts. The story of that long fight, and why we fought, takes up several chapters of this book.

After Carter came Ronald Reagan. A few months after he took office, he faced down striking air traffic controllers by firing them *en masse*. Shortly afterward I marched with hundreds of thousands of union workers on "Solidarity Day," in September 1981, protesting Reagan's brutal union busting. It was the largest mass protest since King's 1963 March on Washington. Reagan ignored it, just as he had ignored an anti-war march and rally of 100,000 on May 3, 1981, in which we opposed his extra-legal intervention in Central America.

Together with many others, I kept organizing, protesting and pressuring against outrageous and illegal government actions through the decades. In the wake of the September 11 attack on the World Trade Center, when President George W. Bush declared "endless war" against terrorists, and falsely claimed that Saddam Hussein's Iraq had "weapons of mass destruction," I helped organize two giant mass protests, one in DC and another in New York. We created millions of flyers and posters which appeared everywhere. We held meetings, issued press releases, and organized endlessly. The protests were so big a NY Times report suggested the anti-war movement represented a "new super-power." Bush called them focus groups, and ignored them.

In mid-2020, as millions mobilized against racist police killings in hundreds of cities across the country, the contrast in the police response with what we witnessed in DC on January 6 was stark. Both the president and the police made it seem the Black Lives Matter protests were the crime, not police violence. Homeland Security troops mobilized to bolster the forces of "law and order." But top military officers saw fit to declare they would not support the president's interventions.

The January 6 *quasi*-insurrection represents a new stage in political life in the United States. We can expect an updated Patriot Act, proscribing all manner of "seditious" activity. The charge of sedition has historically been used mainly against leftwing protesters. The Patriot Act vastly increased surveillance against those who actively oppose U.S. military adventures abroad, and tends to criminalize us. I may be personally liable under the terms of the 2001 Patriot Act, as well as the Sedition Act, passed in 1918, which was used to jail Socialist presidential candidate Eugene V. Debs. His crime was encouraging people to refuse to fight in the first World War. I refused to fight in the Vietnam war, and encouraged thousands of others to do the same. I try to foster resistance to illegal and unjust U.S. military interventions, like those in Iraq and Afghanistan, as well as the ever hotter new cold war against China.

How does all this relate to the Green New Deal, and my claim to be a "Green New Deal revolutionary"? Latest scientific reports make it clear the planet is in mortal danger due to the effects of climate change. Politicians of many stripes have followed the lead of socialist representative Alexandria Ocasio-Cortez in calling for a Green New Deal. While it may not take a political revolution to get a Green New Deal, conversion away from poisonous fossil fuels may only be possible by ending the partnership of big oil and the government, especially the Pentagon. So the effect may be the same. I suggest we'll need a massive social and political transformation to save the planet, as well as to stop endless war.

I feel encouraged that more people than ever see what I see. But many millions more are needed. I hope this book may help convince some of these.

How did an ordinary guy who grew up in a small town in eastern Oregon end up a war resister and a socialist? Back in 1964 I was a Barry Goldwater supporter. Goldwater was a lot like Trump; his running mate was "Bombs Away" Curtis LeMay, whose plan for peace in Vietnam was to "bomb the Vietnamese back to the stone age." After I learned the truth about Vietnam as a student at San Francisco State College in the mid-sixties, I turned against Goldwater, and later Johnson.

It was a stormy time. After McCarthy won the New Hampshire primary that year, President Johnson declared he would not run for a second term as president. The following week Martin Luther King, Jr., was assassinated in Memphis. Then in June, the other anti-war candidate at that time, Bobby Kennedy, was gunned down during his victory speech in California. Later, in August 1968, the storm blew into Chicago for the Democratic National Convention, where anti-war protesters learned first-hand the risks of confronting the powers that be.

From Chicago I caught a ride to Toronto, Canada, where I lived for the next six years, in a kind of shelter from the storm. But as much as I loved and appreciated Canada's more peaceful culture, I ultimately decided to return to the eye of the storm, and continue to work for change. That decision, in 1974, sealed my fate as an organizer for change, determined to stop the war machine and help transform the USA. That has been my quest ever since. I'm so accustomed to it that I feel confident we can literally harness the whirlwind and bring the change we need.

Now we're living in a breakthrough moment. The horrors we witnessed in January 2021 in Washington, DC, marked the end of an epoch. While there will be ripples from that storm, I suggest we are seeing the turning of the tide. The massive Black Lives Matter protests of 2020 mark the beginning of something new: people power strong enough to force real change. But it's important to avoid confusing the new Biden era with the change we seek.

2 – Looking Back to 1968: My Resistance Begins

A person was recently rescued by helicopter after falling 800 feet into the Crater Lake in southern Oregon. In the summer of 1967, when I was part of a crew of forest fire fighters in the nearby Umpqua National Forest, four of us were in a car headed for the Crater Lake resort one night when the war came up in conversation. I said I was against it, and would feel as if I were "on the wrong side" if I went over there. The gung-ho assistant foreman suggested they throw me in the lake. The foreman said "nah – lots of Guardsmen feel the same."

How did a small-town guy from Oregon start thinking iconoclastic thoughts? The following chapters tell my story of rude awakening, exile, and amnesty.

In 1968 the world changed, and I changed forever. I was swept up in a whirlwind. The Tet Offensive[1] in Vietnam exposed the truth about the war: the U.S. could never win because the Vietnamese liberation forces were everywhere in their country and completely fearless. Even before Tet began, in January, I dropped out of San Francisco State College. I wanted to force my small-town draft board to deal with my conscientious objector application instead of insisting that I use a student deferment.

In February I sold my books to get an airplane ticket to Wisconsin, where I joined the anti-war presidential campaign of Eugene McCarthy. In the wake of Tet and the anti-war surge in the primaries at home, President Johnson announced he would not run for re-election. That was late March. A week later the Reverend Martin Luther King, Jr., was shot and killed in Memphis. Spontaneous protests erupted in more than 100 cities across the country. Two months later Bobby Kennedy was shot while giving his victory speech in Los Angeles after winning the Democratic Party primary in California.

I witnessed RFK's assassination on live TV while watching the primary election returns with other McCarthy volunteers at a campaign center in San Francisco. It was the second major shock in two months. Later that week I stuffed some clothes in a suitcase and flew to Washington to help McCarthy's "drive to unify the anti-war forces" at the Democratic National Convention, slated for Chicago in August. I assumed McCarthy would step up and lead. He didn't. When I got to Chicago for the Democratic National Convention, I found the real anti-war forces outside the convention in the streets. I joined them briefly – long enough to witness Mayor Daley's police close in on the protesters and begin bashing heads.

As it became clear to me the war would continue, I headed for Canada. A friend was driving from Chicago to Rochester, New York, and agreed to take me to Canada.

Until then my life was more or less normal: graduate from high school, go to college, meet new people, face new challenges, but normal. Friends at San Francisco State College made me aware of the war in Vietnam. So I watched closely as the Spring 1967 anti-war mobilization marched past my apartment building which faced Golden Gate Park in San Francisco. When a

---

[1] Tet is the name for the Vietnamese lunar new year: in 1968 it fell on January 30. The Vietnamese liberation forces launched a massive campaign of surprise attacks throughout South Vietnam. The offensive shocked U.S. political and military leaders, making it clear their war was unwinnable. (For a brief history of the Vietnamese struggle, see Appendix 1.)

classmate waved me into the flow, I plunged in, marching with the throng that jammed Kesar Stadium. It was the first of many steps that changed my life. Before long I was gathering signatures to get the Peace and Freedom Party on the California ballot. By the semester's end I was writing an application for "C.O. status" – a conscientious objector to the war.

The C.O. application crystallized religious issues for me. A year earlier I was sitting in St. Ignatius Church, which anchored the University of San Francisco – a Jesuit school. A priest who also served as speech professor at USF loudly extolled the "holy war in Vietnam." I got up and walked out, never to return. I had enrolled in USF after leaving the Jesuit seminary in Los Gatos, about an hour and a half south of San Francisco. (I found I did *not* have a vocation to the priesthood, as my nun-teachers had told me for years.) As a land-grant college, USF required all male students to take two years Reserve Officer Training Corps (ROTC) training. Some classmates loved spit-shining their GI shoes and marching in formation in green army suits. But I, like others, didn't want to march – at least not in uniform. That same year, 1966, Phil Ochs launched a whirlwind of anti-ROTC resistance, singing "I ain't marchin' anymore." It was my song.

I had felt lucky to be in San Francisco. As I began to question everything, it was easy to find friends to help me figure things out. I had a work-study scholarship, working in the USF library. A co-worker there was studying at San Francisco State College, and helped me navigate the decision to switch to SF State. I made the transfer the next semester, after spending the summer working with a crew of forest-fire fighters in the wooded mountains of Oregon, where I grew up. The crew's foreman was a National Guardsman who was already starting to question the war. His assistant was another college boy – a footballer – who was gung-ho. I remember four of us were in a car headed for the Crater Lake mountain resort one night when the war came up in conversation. I said I was against the war, and would feel as if I were "on the wrong side" if I went over there. The gung-ho assistant foreman suggested they throw me in the lake. The foreman said "nah – lots of Guardsmen feel the same." (Whew!)

When I returned to San Francisco that fall, the SF State campus was buzzing with anti-war and anti-racist activity. The Black Students Union held daily rallies in the college quadrangle, denouncing the draft as a mechanism to keep white, middle-class boys in school while poor folks, especially Black people, became cannon fodder. I got the message. That's when I started to think about becoming a conscientious objector. Later I figured out that CO status was also a class and race privilege. Later yet, I realized the same about dodging the draft by going to Canada. But it was a process: one new realization led to another. For now, Canada would be my "Plan B" if the McCarthy campaign were not successful in stopping the war.

I should have known, but didn't, that McCarthy wasn't really serious, either about running for president or wanting to stop the war. I came to believe he was a stalking horse – running to make a point without ever really planning to win. Worse yet, his message – "get clean for Gene" – could be deciphered to mean "get off the streets for Gene." He was a safety valve. It worked for a while, at least for me. But 1968 was a special time. Just reflecting on two assassinations that year, not to mention the Tet offensive, should have alerted me. But it took me some time to understand these things.

Of course 1968 didn't emerge "out of nowhere." It was just the year I woke up. I became aware of storms that had passed in recent years while I was still asleep. The Reverend Dr. Martin Luther King, Jr., was killed at a culminating point in the struggle for civil rights which he had led for a decade and a half. He was shot in Memphis while leading a strike of sanitation workers – trying to merge the civil rights struggle with the union movement, a year after his famous speech at Riverside Church condemning the U.S. war in Vietnam, saying "the greatest purveyor of violence in the world is my own government."

That was the year of massive rebellions in the Black communities of Newark and Detroit, two years after the 1965 Watts rebellion in Los Angeles. Malcolm X was killed in 1965, after his message was transformed to condemn not just racism but also imperialism, and to embrace people of all nationalities.

From the viewpoint of the struggle against the U.S. war in Vietnam, the anti-draft resistance was by 1968 morphing into resistance inside the military itself. The American Servicemen's Union (ASU), which later became an important influence for me, was founded by Andy Stapp in 1967. Terry Klug and John Lewis, who later became my close friends and comrades, had gone AWOL (Absent Without Official Leave) from the army that year. By early 1969 they were in the Fort Dix stockade, setting off a new stage in the GI resistance movement. Both John Lewis and another ASU organizer, John Catalinotto, had helped build a very successful "sanctuary" movement in Honolulu for GI resisters. (See Appendix 2.) All these things and much more happened as I was just waking up. They later became enormously important to me.

"Waking up is hard to do," I used to say, quipping on the popular song of the time about breaking up. It was indeed hard, but really emblematic of the time. Later I would comment that if I could do it, others could and would also. As a high school senior in 1964, I had supported the arch-rightist Barry Goldwater against the "peace monger" Lyndon Johnson. When my "modern problems" teacher asked if anyone wanted to vote communist, I, as a clever student, said they already had when they voted for the Democrats.

The distance travelled from 1964 to 1968 was huge for me. It later gave me hope that others could also make the change, even if it was indeed hard to do.

Reflections:

The GI resistance, Civil Rights and Black Liberation movements penetrated my consciousness only gradually at first. I was driven by a need to make personal decisions about how to deal with a war I realized was wrong. As I took this path I came to understand the war itself was part of an even bigger problem, and only a large-scale movement could stop it. Racism, for example, was not obvious to me at that time, since I grew up in a small "cowboy town" in eastern Oregon. I was aware that indigenous people who lived on nearby "Indian reservations" were poor and generally bitter, but I had played Pony League baseball with one of their teams in my early teens, and enjoyed dancing with an Indian girl in high school. I had hiked and vacationed in the stunningly beautiful Wallowa Mountains near my hometown, only learning in a vague way of the heroism of Chief Joseph, who had led his people's war of resistance against white settlers in the mid-1800s, before they were defeated and removed to a barren reservation in northern Idaho, very near the small town of Cottonwood, in the high desert country where I was born. There were few African-American people in the area where I grew up; I heard racist slurs against them, but there was no evidence of the civil rights movement in eastern Oregon at the time; I remained unaware of it. All that changed over time, as I grappled with the challenges of my own resistance.

Leaving the USA in 1968 was seen by some as a kind of "cop out," since all of us were needed to stop the monster. I never thought of it that way. I have always considered all forms of resistance justified, and needed. But I really admired the active duty resisters, and felt inspired to help them however possible. The next stage of my life helped me learn and prepare.

Today's movements for a Green New Deal and for Black Lives Matter are more than a mere echo of 1968. For me they are the return of the whirlwind, with even greater force – and promise for the future.

The Detroit-Windsor Tunnel was my departure point in August of 1968.
I hitched a ride with a friend after the convention meltdown in Chicago,
leaving Mayor Daley and his head-bashing cops behind.[2]

---

[2] See *Chicago '68,* by David Farber; *Chicago: The Whole World is Watching,* Adam Cooper and Nile Southern (eds), with J.C. Gabel and Meg Handler; *Miami and the Siege of Chicago,* by Norman Mailer – among many other sources.

Driving from Chicago following the meltdown of the Democratic Party Convention and the virtual war in the streets outside, we got to Detroit and entered the Windsor Tunnel – the tunnel felt appropriate as an exit from my life in the USA to a new life in Canada. As I left the USA behind, my mind buzzed with questions: What lay ahead for me? What would I do? Who would help me? My friend dropped me in the town of Hamilton, northwest of Niagara Falls, and continued on to Rochester. I bought a one-way ticket to Toronto on a Gray Coach Lines bus – Canada's version of Greyhound.

The bus pulled into Toronto in the early morning. I knew no one there, and had less than a hundred dollars to my name – all of it in my pocket. I found a phone book and looked up "draft resistance." Sure enough, there was a number to call. I dialed the number and heard a sympathetic voice tell me how to get to a counseling center on the subway. By mid-morning I was sitting with a counselor in the office of the Toronto Anti-Draft Programme (TADP), who gave me a copy of the Manual for Draft-Age Immigrants to Canada, and told me I would probably qualify to become a legal immigrant to Canada if I could get a job offer. Meanwhile he sent me to an emergency hostel for new arrivals, and said he would try to place me in the home of supporters who could help me. They were really organized!

The hostel was a little depressing. New arrivals were a bit dazed and uncertain. My main problem was hunger; I noticed there was a nice big kitchen with lots of utensils but no food. So I asked where I could go to get some food, and was directed to a nearby shopping area with dozens of small shops, each specializing in fruit and vegetables, meats, fish, and so on. I brought back enough to feed myself and a few others and cooked up a meal. That seemed to help the general mood a bit.

The next day TADP called to say I had a place to stay with a University of Toronto professor and his family. I was beginning to like TADP quite a lot, and enjoyed reading their Manual for Draft-Age Immigrants to Canada – a professionally produced and very friendly guide created by fellow resisters in the two previous years. Our numbers were growing, and support was strong, thanks to the large Canadian anti-war movement.

My marvelous hosts – a professional couple with two children – fed me and made me feel more than merely welcome, giving me tips on navigating the Toronto subway and buses while I combed through the job ads. Within a week I found a job. I had worked during high school as a grocery clerk back home, so I found a supermarket job. I told the boss I was a draft resister, which was OK with him. So with a "solid job offer," I planned a trip to nearby Buffalo, NY, to then re-enter Canada as a "landed immigrant." In a couple weeks I made this first step in my new country. The job offer made it fairly simple for me to meet the 50-point requirement for immigrant status. Together with some college credit and passable English, I got in much easier than thousands of American military resisters who tried in later years.

I notified my parents in a letter once I was settled. It was the second shocker I gave them that year – the first was a phone call from Madison, Wisconsin, after landing there in February on a flight from San Francisco. It was a lot for them to digest, but after a year or so they planned a visit to Toronto. Meanwhile I wrote them lots of letters, trying to help them understand my viewpoint and decisions. In one letter I suggested the U.S. leadership was like a drunk driver hurtling through a curvy mountain pass in a car full of passengers – risking all our lives and endangering anyone passing by. I felt a duty to try and disable the driver and grab the steering wheel.

Building a life in my new home happened in steps: first I needed some financial help. During the McCarthy presidential campaign I had befriended Bill Johnson, who used his private airplane to carry the candidate to campaign appearances. I begged a loan of $1,000, promising to pay it back in a year. He came through with a check immediately. I was relieved a year later when I paid him back. It was very reassuring to have strong and willing support on both sides of the border. Bill and his friend Sam Brown came to Toronto the next year to enlist exile support for the fall 1969 Moratorium to End the War in Vietnam. We were very glad to see them, but we didn't see much we could do from Canada at that time. Later we saw that an amnesty campaign would be a good anti-war vehicle, but at that moment it felt premature.

After Bill's check arrived I could take my next steps: a rented room and an old car to get me to work. Next, the search for friends and community. There was a constant stream of resisters – "draft dodgers and deserters" – arriving every week. TADP counselors referred me to the Union of American Exiles (UAE), who got together on the University of Toronto campus weekly for camaraderie, mutual advice and support. The conversations ranged from where to get decent cheap food and a place to stay, to what to do about the outrages back home. The U.S. presidential elections were in full swing in the fall of 1968. The UAE debated endorsing Black Panther Eldridge Cleaver's candidacy or supporting Abbie Hoffman's Yippie Party, reminding each other that back in Chicago the Yippies had nominated "Pigasus" (a real pig) as their candidate. We finally agreed to endorse Cleaver and the Black Panthers, and announced it in the UAE newsletter. After "Tricky Dick" Nixon won in November, we started planning for his "in-Hog-uration." (Our battles with Nixon came later. For now he served mainly as justification for our decision to leave the USA.)

Belonging to a group of like-minded resisters was important at every level. First of all, basic necessity: finding people to live with. I met a draft dodger couple from Philadelphia, Charles and Maryanne Campbell, who had found a nice home they were willing to share with me: a cozy house in eastern Toronto's "beaches" neighborhood, close to the shore of Lake Ontario. A charming street car served as public transportation. With three of us cooking, meals were hearty and so was the conversation. As college kids, we gravitated to the Union's newsletter, and gradually became key writers and editors, helping to shape the lively debates in the exile community. We worked closely with the newsletter editor, Stan Pietlock, who was already successful in his transition to Canada, and dedicated himself to smoothing the entry for the rest of us. His gift was to make it fun – we had many enjoyable evenings of endless laughter together, while Stan showed us how to make the newsletter as professional and attractive as possible under the circumstances. He had worked for Newsweek before going north.

The debates revolved around priorities and identity: were we exiles or expatriates, and should we focus on politics or practical matters? I made a ripple with "Some Whiggish Notions," arguing that self-help and mutual support must come first – "first food then politics," to paraphrase Brecht. Not everyone agreed. Heroic martyrdom had some appeal, and for some, the sheer passionate need to express ourselves was vastly more important than mere food and shelter. But a communal Christmas dinner that first chilly year north of the border provided an eloquent reminder of basic priorities, as we pooled resources and "pot-lucked" a turkey with trimmings at our U of T meeting space. I never witnessed a turkey disappear so fast or so completely. The debates raged on again once everyone's belly was full.

Expatriate vs. exile was a hot topic, not always cutting left or right. Many of us were so bitter at the rotten political situation back home that total rejection was the only thing that made sense. So we were expatriates. Others felt "rejected" or criminalized by the war criminals in charge in Washington, and viewed exile as temporary. For many – especially military deserters who by 1969 were showing up in dozens and hundreds – becoming an "expatriate" was not a realistic option. Guys who couldn't get a college deferment either joined the military right out of high school, or were drafted.

So after deserting (or going AWOL – "absent without official leave"), they came to Canada in desperation, and most were not able to put together the combination of qualifying points to get immigrant status. You had to combine education, work experience, money and other factors to make the minimum points to qualify. Without that, deserters could only be temporary visitors, living in a legal limbo. They became the basis for our first significant political struggle in Canada: a campaign to get the Canadian government to "open the doors" to U.S. military deserters.

This campaign found significant support among anti-war Canadian students, who exposed the fact that the government was colluding with the U.S. by refusing legal status to the deserters. The official Canadian government policy was that military status or obligations in a different country would not be considered relevant for people applying for immigrant status. Religious leaders pressed Prime Minister Pierre Trudeau in this campaign, and got him to echo their position that Canada "should be a refuge from militarism," which made a splash in the *Toronto Daily Star*. These words were welcome, but in practice the collusion continued. Anti-war Canadian students blew the government's cover when five different students went to the border posing as a U.S. military deserter and applying for immigrant status. They went to five different border points, and each captured the immigration officers on tape telling him "you can't qualify" as a deserter. This story was picked up by mainstream dailies like the Toronto Star and the semi-official Globe and Mail, and the campaign took off.

By this time "The American Exile in Canada" was in regular publication, and the UAE teamed up with the TADP to build the campaign. Much leadership came from Bill Spira, an intense "Canadian" who was himself a U.S. political expatriate from the anti-communist witch hunt waged by Senator Joe McCarthy in the 1950s. Bill had nominated himself as our "godfather," providing invaluable political savvy and truly fearless leadership. He helped us reach out to religious congregations and prominent individuals – which he had already done to help launch the TADP counseling center a few years earlier. Soon Canada's largest Christian church, the United Church of Canada, together with the Canadian Society of Friends and others, helped spread the word that Canada should indeed be a refuge from militarism, and allow U.S. military deserters to become legal immigrants.

Meanwhile we published reports and editorials in "The American Exile in Canada," and organized letter-writing to the government and parliament to build pressure. This type of campaign had significantly better prospects in

Canada than it would have had in the USA – with about ten percent of the U.S. population, Canadian society was in a sense more neighborly, and the government a bit less distant. And our religious supporters had some genuine clout – more so than their U.S. counterparts.

Within a few months the government announced a "clarification" of its policy, mandating even-handed treatment for U.S. military deserters at the border. We were exultant with victory, but soon had to face the grim reality that "even-handed" treatment would not be enough. As long as our deserter brothers (and their families) had to amass the qualifying points to get immigrant status, in a point system designed to recruit more middle class applicants, the odds were stacked against them.[3] It was a nearly hollow victory, and the flood of deserters coming to Canada became almost a rip tide of AWOL GIs going back home. But many didn't leave Canada, instead opting to continue the underground existence they had been living already for months. And another large percentage did not turn themselves in to military authority on their return to the U.S., instead melting in to semi-underground status either with relatives or in the hundreds of anti-war communities that had sprung up like mushrooms all across the United States in the late 1960s and early 1970s. This was the "Age of Aquarius," and the deserters had a kind of "angel dust," so they could find some protection. Black GIs who went AWOL in many cases got help from sympathetic relatives and friends.

There were tragedies that punctuated the deserters' desperation. Reports of suicides among deserters were frequent. They suffered an extremely precarious existence on the margins of Toronto's youth culture. A few new institutions of self-help and mutual support sprang up. One was called "The Hall," a hangout center where deserters could go for a meal and a referral to a place to stay. They could also watch movies or use The Hall's library to read books, magazines, and an extensive collection of underground newspapers that had flourished on both sides of the border.

One of the mainstay volunteers at The Hall, Jack Colhoun, became an important influence on me and other editors of "The American Expatriate in Canada." (We had changed the newsletter's name to reflect the shift in dominant attitudes, especially among more middle class draft resisters, in our community.) The newsletter had become more and more important for us as

---

[3] The odds are still against today's U.S. military resisters who seek refuge in Canada. Political support has not overcome government rejection.

the months wore on. We had lots to write about, and needed a way to reach out, not only to the broader community of exiled war resisters, but to supporters back home. When I visited The Hall to better understand the reality deserters were facing, I met Jack, who sat me down to talk about what this reality meant, and what we should do about it.

Jack was definitely on the exile side of the debate. A deserter himself, but from an ROTC program at the University of Wisconsin in Madison, where he had recently graduated, he was studying for a doctorate in U.S. history at York University, with plans to return to the USA and teach. Jack's adviser was the well-known anti-war historian Gabriel Kolko, author of *The Roots of American Foreign Policy*, which came out in 1969, as well as numerous other important books, like *The Triumph of Conservatism*, *The Politics of War*, *Anatomy of a War*, *Anatomy of a Peace*, *Century of War*, *Confronting the Third World*, and more. I came to understand why colleagues said Kolko could write books "faster than we can read them" – definitely true in my case.

When Kolko and his wife Joyce invited me over a few weeks later, he personally gave me a copy of *The Roots*, urging me to read it right away in order to clear my mind of liberal confusion. It was worth the short time it took me to read it. They also confided to me that they were ardent supporters of the GI resistance movement, which he characterized as the true "working class anti-war movement." This comment struck me with an impact that only deepened over the years, ultimately having a major influence on my later political thinking and activities. Gabriel and Joyce Kolko had a full partnership: while he was listed as author of all his books, he acknowledged her as a full collaborator, and in some cases, co-author. They were both brilliant and committed anti-imperialists who played a significant role in the anti-war movement.

Jack Colhoun made me think very hard about the "exile vs. expatriate" question, in the context of deserter desperation, as well as the intense political situation in the U.S. He insisted that we should be demanding amnesty, which I had publicly opposed in 1970 when Tom Hayden (co-founder of Students for a Democratic Society, author of the Port Huron Statement, and co-defendant at the famous trial of the Chicago 7) came to an exile conference in Montreal and called on us to demand amnesty as part of the anti-war movement. My editorial in response argued that such a demand would show weakness, not strength, and might be considered a form of tacit recognition of the legitimacy of the war government. This argument may seem silly in retrospect; at the time, however, it reflected the deep and genuine feelings of many war resisters in Canada. But things were changing.

In fact our new life in Canada reflected the continuous change that was the only constant for our generation during the Vietnam years. For me, digging in as a "new Canadian" became a personal project to deepen my political understandings, and to become familiar with people struggling for *better* change in Canada. There was a vibrant Canadian left at that moment. One strand was the leftish "Waffle" movement of the New Democratic Party, which espoused a moderate socialist program. It had a fairly solid following among trade unionists and others. Waffle leaders coined their weird name saying "we'd rather waffle to the left than the right" on issues of Canadian nationalism. I followed their activities and publications closely, became familiar with their discourse and struggles, and joined in at rallies and picket lines.

Further to the left, and more attractive to me, were the editors of *Transformation* magazine (not to be confused with a more recent publication known as "the world's leading transgender life-style magazine," published in Los Angeles for the past 30 years or so). My *Transformation* was a self-published theoretical journal edited by two independent Marxist women – Halley and Maryanne (I forget last names) – who literally took me by the hand and taught me to think like a Marxist. They had dedicated themselves to training new "anti-warriors" like me in the fine points of Marxism. We would sit together for hours reading aloud from Mao Zedong's *Four Essays on Philosophy*, discussing the intricacies of dialectical materialism as applied to planning for revolution. We also read Friedrich Engels' *Origin of the Family, Private Property and the State*, which became a cornerstone text for me alongside *The Communist Manifesto*, as well as Lenin's *State and Revolution*, and *What Is to Be Done?* This was a deeply transformative education for me, which has formed the basis of my thinking ever since that time: I became a Marxist and socialist.

The logical next step was to try to become involved with Canadian workers. This search brought me back to Bill Spira, the war resister expatriates' "godfather," who had to some extent lost faith in me due to my participation in the activities of the Union of American Exiles. He disapproved because he always counseled us to "blend in" as new Canadians. But when he listened to my new-found Marxist thinking, he had just the right thing for me: working with him as an organizer for a Canadian textile workers union. I would be the "inside guy" while he worked with me on home visitations from outside. So that's what we did: I got myself hired to work at the Puretex factory not far from my first supermarket job in Toronto's northern suburb, where I could get to know the workers, and talk up the union – the Canadian Textile and Chemical Union. This union was led by passionate reds, completely independent of Canada's affiliate of the AFL-CIO, but allied with a Canadian federation of independent unions. They were hard working, inspired organizers, and our collaboration bore fruit.

The Puretex workers were mainly recent Italian immigrants, about 80 percent women and 20 percent men. As first generation immigrants, they retained their political views from the old country: mainly leftist and pro-union. So winning their support for a union was not hugely difficult: we just had to get their home addresses and visit them. They welcomed us, and after listening to our union spiel, they would serve coffee or wine and tell their stories, not only of the bad conditions at the Puretex factory, but also in Italy. And "yes," they would say, "a union is what we need." For me it was a living textbook in organizing: copying people's car license plate numbers, searching for their addresses, visiting their homes, and then forming a secret inside committee of potential union leaders and activists.

It wasn't always easy, of course, and we made at least one costly mistake: trying to convince a young woman who worked in the company office to join us. She was against it, which annoyed Bill, who said something like "just wait, you'll come around before long." I did not recall a threatening tone at the time, but a few nights later I was confronted as I left the plant by the girl's boyfriend and his buddies, who jumped me and gave me a good beating. Only the fact that they pulled my coat over my head prevented serious head injuries. They mainly meant to scare me, which they did. I had already been transferred to the night shift after a foreman got wind of my "double duty," so my effectiveness in the plant was pretty much finished. I suggested to Bill that I should quit and let the long-term workers take over. The women leaders were ready, and soon they mounted a large-scale public campaign for union recognition, which they won, after months of struggle.

Bill reluctantly agreed to let me go, disappointed that I would not stay the course. It was especially disappointing for him that my friend Jack had convinced me that I should work for "Amex" full-time so we could develop a major campaign for amnesty. ("Amex" was our new name for The American Exile/Expatriate in Canada – finessing the identity debate.)

My first three years in Canada were deeply transformative for me. "Coming of age" is a major transition under any circumstances, and in some ways my circumstances were ideal. I really liked Canada. I was happy to have found many interesting friends, and was able to get back into college, despite other priorities. It was hard to stay focused on undergraduate studies while involved in a major, transformative learning experience that included helping others for whom the life changes were overwhelming. And while I had very little money and was struggling in college, I was learning every day.

My transition to Marxist thinking was definitely the big thing for me, largely thanks to my Canadian friends and the new environment. But the most important influence for me was Ho Chi Minh and the Vietnamese liberation movement. The 1968 Tet chant rang true: "Ho, Ho, Ho Chi Minh, Vietnam is gonna win!" I read and re-read Ho's biography, and everything I could get my hands on about Vietnam. For me there was no question: "our side" was the Vietnamese side. The other side was the enemy in Washington. Ho was the ultimate patriot, declaring that for a colonized country like Vietnam, "patriotism is applied internationalism." Ho made it clear that for those of us living in imperialist countries, our duty was international solidarity, and rejection of false imperialist "patriotism." Since the leading "patriot" in the USA was war criminal Nixon, it wasn't too difficult for me to figure it out.

In late 1970 I met a young woman, Carol Woolverton, who became my partner and lifelong friend. Our relationship was solid for four years in Toronto. She made me more "Canadian" – teaching me to ice skate, sharing her family with me, asking for help while she struggled with college. We decided to return together to the USA in 1974, after draft refusal charges against me were dismissed on a technicality two years earlier. We got married at a chapel in Reno after visiting my parents in Oakland and then hitchhiked to a July 4 VVAW (Vietnam Veterans Against the War) demonstration in Washington, DC.

Our wedding was opportunistic: we wanted U.S. immigration status for Carol, and getting married was the easiest way to get it. While the stresses of "re-entry" and my immaturity doomed our long-term prospects, we remained life-long friends and comrades after separating in late 1975. We had traveled together to Portugal to witness the revolution there, and she decided to stay a while longer. When she returned a year later, she was pregnant and needed some help. I was more than willing, so despite her anger at me she let me share some parenting chores for her beautiful baby, Jonas, who remains my "godson" to this day. Carol died of cancer in 2010.

Reflections:

My decision to refuse the draft and leave the USA for Canada was life-changing and formative. It was the beginning of a life quest that has been never-ending. Instead of pursuing a normal career, I have dedicated most of my life to constant efforts to learn about and "change the world." In the process I "missed out" on some aspects of a "normal life," opting instead for a variety of adventures which were all in pursuit of the elusive goal of change. There have been few shining moments, and numerous unfortunate setbacks. But the quest continues. Along the way I have sustained a sense of "revolutionary optimism," that I am part of a widening and deepening stream of expanded consciousness about new and better possibilities.

I think a long view helps. Back in the sixties and seventies there was a sense of urgency about change, followed by frustration at shortcomings and setbacks. But the amazing success of our struggle for amnesty, together with the defeat of Nixon, who was forced to resign in disgrace in 1974, have served as examples and reminders for me that change is possible, and that solidarity and perseverance can lead to encouraging breakthroughs. This fostered over-optimism following the exhilarating triumph of Vietnam's liberation forces in 1975. I started to believe in the discredited "domino theory," and looked for a steady succession of new anti-imperialist victories around the world, and to a long "springtime" of progressive thinking at home. So the tidal wave of post-Vietnam reaction ushered in by Ronald Reagan in 1980, which has raged unabated ever since, caught me by surprise. (Reagan dedicated his presidency to overcoming the "Vietnam Syndrome" – a widespread reluctance among people in the USA to engage in more Vietnam-style interventionist adventures.)

I have never ceased to be optimistic, and I stubbornly continue to believe that the force of solidarity and struggle is the force of life itself, and that it will prevail.

The resurgence of struggle, both in the streets and the ballot box, brought on by Bernie Sanders, AOC, and the COVID19 pandemic and related depression, feels to me like springtime after a long winter.

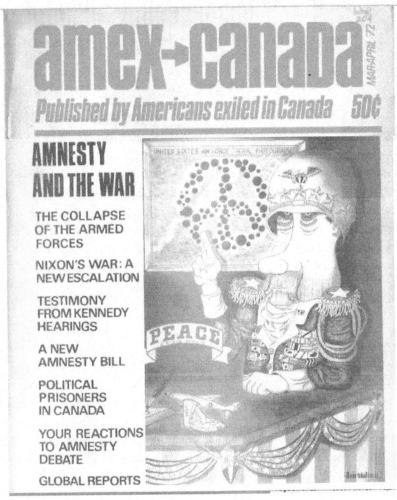

The March-April 1972 issue of Amex-Canada.
Editorial appears in Appendix 3. (Amex graphic by Don Zielinski)

It should not have been difficult to figure out the amnesty issue, but it was. Part of the problem was emotional; another was social. And the political part was complicated. Emotionally, we were so angry at the U.S. government that it was repugnant to "ask" for anything. Socially, we were concerned about alienating our friends who felt as we all did about it. And many resisters worried that a campaign for amnesty would offend Canadians who had welcomed us. Politically, we came to know amnesty was right, but we had to find a way to say it.

At a press conference in Toronto Jan. 17, 1972: "a group of American draft dodgers and deserters rejects 'alternative service' as a condition for amnesty and calls for a 'totally non-punitive restoration of civil liberties' if and when they return home to the U.S. The group, said to represent between 70,000 and 100,000 fellow exiled Americans in Canada, includes: (l to r) Dave Beauchene, N.H.; Dick Burroughs, Texas; Dee Knight, Calif.; Dick Brown, Mich.; Jack Colhoun, N.Y.; Larry Martin, Calif.; Patrick Cook, Kansas."
Canadian Press photo

How could we say we demand amnesty from a cabal of war criminals? How could we say to people we felt should be in jail, that they should not prosecute us? In a way, it was an example of "applied dialectical materialism" – an understanding that things change. The losers now would indeed be later to win, as Bob Dylan had sung in "The Times They are a-Changin'." That thought made it easier to figure out. We did not need to ask for anything – even if the liberal politicians tried to make it seem that way. There was a gulf between them and us. We were proud of our resistance, and defiant about claiming the rightness of our position. We weren't asking for favors or forgiveness.

There was nothing to forgive. We had done the right thing. The government was wrong. Simple. We decided that if we were to wage a campaign we would have to call it amnesty, but we would insist that it be universal and unconditional.

All this was in response to the "conditional amnesty" proposals of various liberal politicians.

Most important was the "universal" part. The liberal politicians hoped they could "forgive" draft resisters while leaving military resisters and veterans to the military, and completely forgetting about other anti-war activists who were either in jail or subject to prosecution. We refused to see any differences based on timing or intensity of opposition. The war was the crime. Resistance was right and necessary. No punishment could be considered acceptable.

We found a mood in the media that was surprisingly open to us. The anti-war movement held high political ground at that moment. Hundreds of thousands of people had mobilized and marched all across the USA and the world. Draft boards had been flooded with CO applications. Judges were dismissing draft cases by the dozens. My own case was dismissed on a technicality in the spring of 1972.

In 1970, Marine Colonel Robert Heinl published an article saying the U.S. military was "breaking down" in Vietnam. Soldiers were refusing to fight. Junior officers and "gung-ho" sergeants were being "fragged." (Fragmentation grenades rolled into their tents at night...) Bluntly stated, the U.S. was losing the war. The Vietnamese liberation forces were winning. "I ain't-a-marchin' anymore," had become "we don't want your fucking war!"

I was chosen to be spokesperson at the January 1972 Toronto press conference. (I had relatively short hair.) It was a mixed blessing. Being "pumped up," I spoke a little more than necessary. Nobody objected, but afterwards I felt it would have been better for others to speak more. The results were good anyway. Media coverage got it fairly close to right: "Vietnam resisters want amnesty with no apology." "Resisters tell Nixon: amnesty for all with no conditions."

The coverage made it clear that amnesty had to be *universal:* for military deserters and veterans just as much as for draft resisters. This was crucial: deserters were suffering more than draft resisters, and veterans with bad discharges carried a stigma for life. In both cases they faced military "justice," often harsher than the civilian version. And their resistance inside the military had become the cutting edge. Anti-war activists facing arrests or already in jail also had to be included. Making these points was the main reason we had decided to enter the amnesty debate in the first place – along with assuring that amnesty would be at its core an *anti-war* issue, rather than a humanitarian one.

Following the press conference our phones lit up. We had a constant stream of interviews that continued steadily through the ensuing years until President Carter finally declared a weak substitute for amnesty in January 1977. We then determined that was the extent of what could be won at that time. It was not universal, because military resisters were still required to be processed out of the military through an administrative procedure. But we assessed that the procedure was not punitive and was predictably brief, and thousands of deserters took advantage of it. Veterans with less-than-honorable discharges were still forced to grapple with an opaque and thoroughly unjust appeal procedure to take their chances, which were always slim. We vowed to continue the fight alongside veterans on this issue.

We had a slogan – *Amnesty for the future, not just the past.* It meant we were calling for the right to resist unjust wars: present, past and future.

As we waged the campaign from Toronto following the January 1972 press conference, we pulled together a group of resisters who came from cities and towns across the USA, who were willing to be interviewed by local media people from the U.S. This was a good tactic: we were not speaking *for* anyone, but helping hometown reporters find "local boys" and their wives, who could tell their own stories.

The January 1972 press conference was just the beginning. It galvanized us as Amex editors to set forth a position and build a movement around it. Jack and I co-authored a detailed position paper explaining what Universal, Unconditional Amnesty meant. *(See Appendix 3.)* Then we called meetings and conferences to organize for it. The most important effect was to bring other leaders to join our struggle. In a June 1972 conference at the Canadian Society of Friends, Gerry Condon and Sandy Rutherford showed up – a couple who became our partners in a long-term campaign.

I had first met Gerry in 1965 at the University of San Francisco. While I moved on to SF State and then the McCarthy campaign, Gerry left USF and signed up for the Green Berets. While I was campaigning for McCarthy or demonstrating on the streets of Chicago, Gerry had begun to speak out against the Vietnam War at Fort Bragg and to refuse military orders. The Army ordered him to deploy to Vietnam and he refused. He was court-martialed and got a sentence of ten years' hard labor and a dishonorable discharge (so-called). At that point he somehow escaped from Fort Bragg, headed to Montreal, and from there went to Sweden. He became active with the American Deserters Committee there, toured Europe, made contact with resisters in France and Germany, and met Sandy, who was just as militant as he was. When they got wind of the amnesty campaign, they came to Canada, showing up at our 1972 spring conference at the Friends Meeting House in Toronto. There is much more to tell about Gerry, as we'll see later. He has devoted his life to the struggle of military resisters and veterans, and has been a long-time leader of Veterans For Peace.

Gerry and Sandy were special. They signed on. Even though they were headed to Vancouver, on Canada's west coast, they became part of the nucleus of our campaign, which was already international: spanning Canada, the U.S., and Europe.

Later that year another couple arrived in Toronto: Steve Grossman and Evangeline Mix Lantana. Desperate for rest and some personal security after months living underground in Ohio, their timing was bad: the Canadian government was in the process of putting a hold on immigration applications. Steve and Evangeline motivated us to become part of another campaign – this time for "immigration amnesty" in Canada.

This "immigration amnesty" issue wasn't really *our* campaign, since Amex had become the voice of the American "exiles" demanding amnesty in the USA, in contrast to American "expatriates" who wanted to sink roots in Canada and try to forget about the United States. This immigration amnesty represented a need of the Canadian government to resolve a problem, since there were many thousands of U.S. military deserters and war resisters living underground in Canada, as well as underground immigrants from other countries.

Our friends at TADP and the other war resister counseling centers across Canada led the "immigration amnesty" campaign. Dick Brown, one of the TADP counselors, can be credited with kicking it off. He wrote a letter to the Canadian government saying the situation of thousands of underground deserters and resisters needed to be resolved. Amazingly, the Canadian government took Brown's suggestion seriously. It seems there was a magic moment, in which Canadian authorities considered it best in relation to their "friends" in Washington, DC, to stop "hiding" a group of U.S. felons. A whole network of our supporters mobilized, from TADP and Bill Spira to the United Church of Canada, Quakers, Mennonites, the New Democratic Party and others. This was an idea whose time had come. Amex supported it wholeheartedly – even if we were not included in the planning.

By late 1973 the campaign for immigration amnesty was successful, and the victory was sweet. In the course of that campaign, Steve and Evangeline had become indispensable core members of the Amex leadership team, and now they were legal immigrants in Canada. Their later contribution to the struggle for amnesty was incalculably great. And we became life-long friends and comrades.

Amex now had its leadership core: Jack, myself, Gerry, Sandy, Steve and Evangeline. This crew took the amnesty struggle through to its culmination in 1977. I was not in the core leadership after 1974, because I had relocated to New York, but was still considered part of the Amex core until sometime in 1975, when I made a mistake under pressure from the liberal wing of the amnesty movement. But all that is part of what happened next.

Reflections:

The shift from an "expatriate" to "exile" mentality was easier for me than some others because of the political aspect. Like most others in our war resister community, I was happy in Canada, content to make a new life and leave the stresses we faced in "the old country" back there. But I remained a committed anti-imperialist, and was moving even further left. So it was easy to convince me to wage an anti-imperialist campaign for amnesty. It made sense politically. We could deliver a strong message, and in the process help fellow resisters who really needed to return home, as well as other resisters who had never left the USA.

But we faced some flack. A lot of the resisters who had settled into Canada preferred not to be involved, or even be reminded or "implicated" in the amnesty campaign. For some it seemed we were ungrateful to Canada, which wasn't true, but was a real concern. Others just felt it brought up bad memories, or caused political discomfort. Counselors at TADP and their counterparts in other Canadian cities had been trained to carefully avoid politics, and we were "rubbing their noses in it." Some friendships were strained because of this. But others were strengthened. A lot of resisters really needed amnesty. It became a fight for a future they had been afraid to hope for.

Fighting for your rights was part of the "new normal" of that time. Now it's coming back with a vengeance.

5 – 1972: An International Campaign

The year 1972 was another whirlwind: constant new developments, media interviews, late nights talking and planning, meetings to plan more meetings or conferences, and much more. The new Amex leadership group learned a lot "on the fly" about organizing. Amex had become the hub of an international campaign for universal, unconditional amnesty. We were also deeply involved in the global anti-war movement.

We forged a strategic alliance with the Vietnam Veterans Against the War (VVAW). Resisters and veterans were inevitably pitted against each other by the media and even more so by politicians. We knew better. Veterans and active duty GIs felt in their guts and bones what we had figured out slightly earlier: the government was lying to us and bludgeoning our generation to be cannon fodder in their criminal war, supposedly against communism, but really for profits and domination. We knew the experience had been much harder for the vets. They carried physical and emotional injuries that would not heal. Not all of them could figure it out enough to find solidarity with resisters. But the best of them could, and were incredibly good. Our alliance with them was very powerful politically.

There were political challenges to figure out. We had to explain how and why *all* types of resisters should get amnesty. Not just draft resisters. Not just deserters. The anti-war movement both at home and in Vietnam was in a fierce confrontation against the brutal and criminal U.S. war machine. Our generation, Black, Latinx and white, witnessed and was victim to massive violent criminal actions by local, state and federal governments. The violence in Vietnam had an echo in brutal repression against civil rights and anti-war activists across the country – and righteous rebellions in response. Many of us believed that Malcolm X, Martin Luther King, Jr., and Robert Kennedy had all been gunned down as "enemies of the state." Dozens of Black Panther Party members had been executed, most of them on the streets. Following Dr. King's assassination, mass rebellions exploded in more than 100 cities.

The horrific, senseless slaughter in Vietnam stimulated ever more passionate and intense opposition at home. The resistance escalated fast: burning draft cards became passé as draft *boards* burned. Reserve Officer Training Corps (ROTC) centers burned on some campuses. The entire U.S. military machine faced mass mutiny in Vietnam, where "fragging" of officers and non-commissioned officers had reached epidemic proportions. The anti-war movement had become a "war against the war."

Karl Armstrong came to Toronto to live underground, exactly a month after our January 1972 press conference. We had just called for "a totally non-punitive restoration of civil liberties for all persons charged ... or convicted ... due to actions relating directly or indirectly to the Indochinese war." Karl was accused of bombing the Army Math Research Center in Madison, Wisconsin, in August 1970. He and his brother Dwight were charged with first-degree murder, because a researcher working late on the night of the bombing died as a result of the action. Karl and Dwight personified the level of anti-war opposition in the U.S. at the time. Our focus was on Karl, since his brother did not come to Toronto.

There was no question that we would defend Karl Armstrong. He was one of us. However, his case was more about extradition than amnesty. Our friends at TADP took the lead. Karl had contacted them on arrival. They stepped up, first with safe housing, then by organizing his defense against extradition as a political fugitive. My roommate at the time, John Liss, a former TADP counselor, had recently passed the bar to practice law in Toronto. He was working with Clayton Ruby, who together with Paul Copeland had provided legal support to TADP for several years.

The defense team brought prominent U.S. anti-war activists to Toronto to testify at the extradition hearing. Tom Hayden, Noam Chomsky and the well-known pacifist Staughton Lynd all testified for Karl. They made it clear his actions were part of a long campaign to shut down a major cog in the U.S. war machine. These leaders, all known for non-violent protest, vouched for Karl's peaceful intentions. They insisted the bombing was a last resort, and the death of the researcher was an accident, the result of a misguided but understandable tactic.

None of it mattered. Karl was ordered to be extradited on June 30, 1972. Nine months later he was handed over to U.S. authorities and returned to Madison to face trial for murder and arson. The judge could hear demonstrators outside court shouting "Free Karl Armstrong!" Eventually Karl was convicted of second-degree murder and arson, and sentenced to 23 years in prison, which was reduced on appeal to seven years. One of TADP's long-time counselors, Naomi Wall, married Karl while he was in prison, which seemed to help his chances of parole. Released on parole in 1980, he continued to live in Madison where he operated a set of fruit drink stands on the campus mall for years.

Karl Armstrong's case, and the thousands of cases of militant GI resisters in Vietnam and at military bases across the U.S. and around the world, dramatized for us the critical need for *universal,* as well as unconditional amnesty. Take the following examples.

My life-long friend and comrade Terry Klug returned from exile in Paris in January 1969 on what he thought would be a "deal" for light treatment. He was grabbed at Kennedy Airport and whisked to the stockade at Fort Dix, New Jersey. As an active member of the American Servicemen's Union (ASU), he immediately set about organizing resistance in the oppressively overcrowded stockade, which was rife with racism and violent abuse. It was not long before the stockade burned to the ground in a massive rebellion. Terry was one of several organizers charged with aggravated arson, insubordination, mutiny, etc., etc. – in addition to desertion. The court martial failed to convict him of anything but desertion, so Terry and the other organizers "dodged a bullet" of 50-plus years' hard labor. But Terry still went to the Fort Leavenworth Stockade for 17 months and got a dishonorable discharge. He and many others – of whom there were hundreds if not thousands at bases across the country – spent years behind bars, and have carried that bad paper and the stigma that goes with it for the rest of their lives.

Miraculously, Terry managed to forge a good life, with good union jobs, in spite of the stigma. (The "mirade"? Rock-solid political and moral support from his brothers in the ASU, and Workers World Party which stood behind the ASU.) Many others were not so lucky.

There were more than half a million "bad paper vets" from the Vietnam era. The bad discharges piled on top of Post-Vietnam Stress (PVS) syndrome (later designated as Post *Traumatic* Stress Disorder, or PTSD). Now a lost generation of Vietnam-era veterans lives a permanent nightmare: mass unemployment, homelessness, mental illness, prison and suicide at epidemic proportions. A 2016 VA report said that out of 55 million veterans from 1979 to 2014, an average of 20 veterans a day have died from suicide. That computes to more than a quarter million suicides during that period. An estimated total of between 150,000 and 200,000 *Vietnam* veteran suicides makes about triple the official number of U.S. combat deaths in Vietnam.

Meanwhile, by 1988, more than half of all Vietnam veterans diagnosed with PTSD reported they had been arrested, more than a third of them multiple times. In 1985, more than one in five prison inmates in the U.S. was a veteran. What was their crime? Was PTSD a crime? More to the point, what was their life like? Constant nightmarish flashbacks, often causing violent reactions and broken homes leading to life on the streets, have made Vietnam veterans permanent war victims.

This was the background as we launched our amnesty campaign. We started by looking for allies and mentors. We found two groups with ongoing amnesty campaigns: the Southern Conference Educational Fund (SCEF), based in Louisville, Kentucky, and Safe Return, in New York. They could not have been more different.

Our first effort tapped into three legends: SCEF director Carl Braden – famous for standing up to the House Un-American Activities Committee and going to jail for it – and Virginia Collins, Vice President of the Republic of New Africa. Virginia was also a national board member of the Women's International League for Peace and Freedom (WILPF). The two were conducting a national amnesty speaking tour on behalf of Virginia's son Walter Collins.

Walter had already spent 16 months of five concurrent five-year maximum sentences in federal prison for draft resistance. Not *just* a draft resister, he was also the regional director of the National Association of Black Students (NABS) and a founder of the National Black Draft Counselors. Walter had been working on a Ph.D. thesis at the University of Michigan when his draft board cancelled his student deferment and classified him 1-A. Within two weeks of reclassification, the draft board ordered Walter's induction. He fought it, refusing induction five times, but the draft board was determined to stop him. At the age of 27 he

Walter Collins

was a veteran civil rights organizer. He had participated in the 1963 sit-ins to desegregate lunch counters and theaters in New Orleans, and had helped

Carl Braden and Virginia Collins

register voters in Louisiana and Mississippi, in the 1964 Mississippi Freedom Summer Project. Beyond that, as a SCEF organizer he had helped form a Black-white alliance of workers in the Masonite Corporation in Laurel, Miss. According to Braden, who told the story as part of the national speaking tour, Walter's work led to a successful woodcutters strike.

Braden said the strike's Black-white unity "was, in a large part, due to the work of Walter Collins."

Carl and Virginia's campaign, covering 42 states, kept Walter safe while he was in prison, and also dramatized the demand for amnesty for all war resisters and political prisoners. Black prisoners were under the gun at that time: in the fall of 1971 New York Governor Nelson Rockefeller crushed a prisoner rebellion at Attica State Prison in western New York, killing dozens; and Black Panther leader George Jackson was killed at San Quentin State Prison in California two months earlier.

We invited Carl Braden to come to Toronto to give us the benefit of their experience. Together with TADP we organized a meeting that drew about 50 resisters. Carl explained how we could build an effective campaign for amnesty, highlighting all the political issues. He also sat down with me personally to talk about his life as an organizer. He was a powerful inspiration to me. He and his wife Anne had devoted their lives to fighting racism. In 1954 they bought a home in an all-white neighbor-hood in Louisville, and then deeded it to an African-American family. The Ku Klux Klan responded by stoning and firing shots at the house, burning a cross in front of it, and then setting off explosives under it, driving the family out and destroying the home. Both Carl and Anne were charged with "sedition," since working for racial integration at that time was generally considered communist subversion. The Klan terrorists were not charged; Carl was convicted and sentenced to 15 years in prison. He served seven months of his sentence before he was released on bond pending appeal. His conviction was then overturned, so he got out and continued organizing.

The campaign for Walter Collins succeeded. Out of jail by spring 1973, Walter participated in our amnesty organizers' conference. Both he and his mother became original board members of the National Council for Universal Unconditional Amnesty later that year. What I learned from Walter was invaluable, since I had never really experienced the epic struggles against racism and segregation that had defined his and his mother's lives. He was among the first to show me that resisting the draft was part of a vastly deeper struggle. While the Black Students Union at San Francisco State College had made me understand the draft as part of a system that protects privileges of class and race, Walter's life work – as a founding organizer of the Student Non-Violent Coordinating Committee (SNCC), and all the rest – showed a quiet determination that was genuinely fierce and implacable. We had a talk at one point that hit me hard. He stated bluntly that no white person in America could be free of racism. He made it clear that this was true regardless of what I or any other white person might think or feel. Painful and troubling as it was to hear, I had to accept it, knowing that, in my case at least, growing up blind to the prejudice and systemic racism that was as common as air elsewhere, had left me unaware of most of what Walter was trying to tell me. It was a relief to know he was telling me this to help open my eyes and heart, so I might be better able to fight and organize for change. Maybe I could get to the level of Carl Braden – after a lifetime or two of tireless organizing! Walter died of cancer in 1995.

About a month after Carl Braden's visit, I received a surprise letter – my indictment for refusing the draft had been dismissed on a technicality, through no effort on my part. (It's possible supporters in Oregon did something – I had received an award from peace activists the year before.) Suddenly I was free to return to the U.S. By this time it didn't mean, for me at least, that I would go home. But I could travel back and forth at will.

This freedom to travel opened up some possibilities in our efforts to build an amnesty movement. I could meet *directly* with potential allies. The first task was reaching out to push for total amnesty with anti-war presidential candidate George McGovern, who was running against Nixon in 1972. This was a little bit like *déjà vu* for me, since I had lived the futility of Eugene McCarthy's run in 1968. But in our discussions in the Amex leadership group, we determined that getting McGovern to support *true* amnesty – universal and unconditional – would be huge. And even if he didn't go "all the way," or if it took a while, educating him and his supporters would be a critical part of our overall strategy. I travelled to California in May: McGovern's campaign was at high tide ahead of the June primary election there. We hoped I could get the candidate to declare his support for us. But he was moving in the other direction. Still, I made some contacts, and some plans to press more aggressively at the Democratic Party convention in Miami that August.

Meanwhile we mounted a speaking tour – I and other members of the anti-war exile community who could travel legally in the U.S. We used the debate on amnesty to clarify and personify our positions. We went wherever we could get bookings. A series of public meetings and media interviews took place in Philadelphia and nearby Wilmington, Delaware. On one TV show I debated amnesty and the war with an army colonel. (He was a little surprised that I could counter all his rebuttals.) We also made stops in Iowa, Ohio, upstate New York, and California. Wherever we visited we developed support, and managed to deepen the understanding of universal, unconditional amnesty.

This campaign was important: we were continuously establishing credibility as spokespeople for war resisters in exile. We were also showing that grassroots support was strong for our cause. And we were developing our capacity for organizing and campaigning. All these things became even more important in the course of the year as we moved to forge alliances and coalitions. I also visited New York City, for meetings with key supporters, which began the process of forging the National Council for Universal Unconditional Amnesty.

In New York I also met with Todd Ensign and Michael Uhl of Safe Return, a kind of left-legal partnership that was building support for amnesty. They shared our anti-war politics, and wanted us to join them in a series of dramatic actions designed to force amnesty. These two people in an office on Fifth Avenue in New York had a knack for media-oriented confrontational tactics. In March of 1972, they brought Army deserter John David Herndon back to the U.S. from his exile in Paris. When Herndon got off the plane at Kennedy airport, he was arrested immediately, with TV cameras rolling and reporters calling out questions.

This tactic became a sort of Safe Return trademark. We were not involved in that action, but I visited Safe Return when I went to New York shortly afterward. They wanted Amex to help with similar dramatic confrontations they were planning. They invited me to join them in "surfacing" deserter Tom Michaud on the floor of the 1972 Democratic Party convention in Miami. That potentially brilliant tactic fizzled. Authorities swiftly hustled Michaud off to a Marine Corps brig, with very little attention paid by convention delegates or national media.

That experience chilled our enthusiasm for attempting dramatic media events – even though we succeeded with something similar on a larger scale four years later at the 1976 Democratic National Convention in New York. But a lot had to happen before then.

The most exciting thing that happened in Miami, for me, was meeting, marching, and protesting with VVAW in the streets outside the conventions. VVAW had no faith in McGovern, believing only in their own efforts to stop the war and get justice. Alliance with VVAW became the key for us to whatever broader coalition we would form. Despite differences in timing and direct personal experience, we had a very tight bond: we were fighting to redress a crime that had been committed against us.

From this background we moved to form a new coalition: the National Council for Universal Unconditional Amnesty. Our bond with VVAW made it difficult for less forthright supporters to "water down" our demands. Of course we wanted and needed liberal support, and got it. Allies included the National Council of Churches, which had sponsored anti-draft counseling centers on both sides of the border; the American Civil Liberties Union, which provided some legal help to resisters alongside numerous other sources of legal support (and also helped us find financial support); and the War Resisters League, which supported resisters in general even when they had to stretch their pacifist principles to find common cause with all the various types of resistance that emerged against the U.S. war in Vietnam.

None of these groups except VVAW (the best of them) shared our recognition of the Vietnamese National Liberation Front as "our side" against the "enemy" in Washington. But the anti-war dynamic brought them to us like a magnet. Even if they wanted us to be victims they could support and rescue, they still found themselves compelled to recognize the right of our resistance, and to support our reasonable demand for universal unconditional amnesty. Our tight alliance with VVAW also assured that amnesty supporters had little choice but to stand with our formulation: *universal and unconditional amnesty* – to include military resisters, veterans and hard-core activists. Nothing less would be acceptable.

Reflections:

Going back to the U.S. – "home" – seemed both weird and exciting. I felt both a thrill and a mix of other feelings. We had turned our back on "the old country" and all its self-destructive craziness. Now I was digging in as if I had never left. Some of our friends in Canada had mixed feelings at best. My parents knew I wasn't really "back," and even some of the McGovern campaigners looked at me as if I were a foreigner. But I wasn't. As we toured the country, we got "welcome home" a lot. And my meetings with amnesty supporters were encouraging: we could do this.

There was a search underway in the USA back then – a search for a path out of the nightmare of war and racism. It turned into a labyrinth as Nixon brought back the anti-communist *COINTELPRO* campaigns of the McCarthyite 1950s. That reaction has lasted until now. That's the reaction we're up against today. While many saw Trump as something new, I have seen him as the latest version of a long-lasting reaction that may be breathing its last. We need to make that dream come true!

6 – 1973: A Weird Way of Making Peace

As 1972 was ending, Nixon and Kissinger had a weird way of making peace. Kissinger declared "peace is at hand" on the eve of the November 1972 elections – assuring anyone who wanted to believe that Nixon was delivering "peace with honor," and heading off "peace" votes for the hapless McGovern. (McGovern's campaign was so weak and pathetic it raised suspicions – for me at least – of the same "stalking horse" role that Eugene McCarthy had run four years earlier.) Peace negotiations had dragged on ever since the 1968 Tet Offensive made it clear the U.S. could not win. During that time Nixon had actually expanded the war with criminal bombing raids into Cambodia, hoping in vain to destroy the legendary Ho Chi Minh Trail. And he continued to carpet bomb North Vietnam, while napalm and Agent Orange rained down on the jungles of South Vietnam, supposedly bolstering the pathetic puppet forces of his "Vietnamization" strategy.

We knew the war was ending – GIs on the ground in Vietnam had stopped fighting altogether. Now mutinies were happening on aircraft carriers, and even bomber pilots were refusing to fly. But Nixon and Kissinger had a "last hurrah" – the Christmas bombing of 1972. They apparently figured if they could pull off a massive bombing campaign against North Vietnam before signing a peace agreement, they might be able to call the outcome a victory. The ploy backfired: Vietnamese anti-aircraft guns took out about a third of the U.S. B52 fleet with SAM3 surface-to-air missiles. That's how 1972 ended.

The Paris Peace Accords took center stage in January 1973. Treaty signing was set for January 27. We accepted an invitation from Safe Return to co-sponsor an "International Conference of Exiles for Amnesty" in Paris during the week after the peace treaty would be signed. We saw significant potential for the conference as an opportunity to unify American exile groups in Canada, France, Sweden and England (plus GIs based in Germany), while meeting with American supporters and kicking off the amnesty campaign in a major way. Things turned out a bit differently. Shortly after our delegation from Canada landed in Paris we learned that Nixon had pressured French President Georges Pompidou into banning the conference. Next we learned that our Safe Return co-sponsors had unilaterally cancelled their participation in the conference. Would-be participants from the U.S. not already in transit were told to stay in New York. We got a rude awakening to the realities and risks involved in pulling off high profile international conferences.

Amex did not agree with canceling the conference. We liked the advice of French supporters to convene it "underground." But it was delicate. Rumor held that French police had staked out our hotel, to arrest and deport anyone who tried to convene the conference. We did not want to put our fellow exiles at risk, but we were also loath to let Nixon stop us. So we pulled together a series of meetings with delegates from VVAW, exiles from Sweden, France, and Great Britain, as well as a GI and some GI organizers from RITA Act in West Germany ("RITA" was an acronym for Resistance In The Army). We still had plenty of support in France. A group of sympathetic French intellectuals called a press conference to denounce Pompidou's capitulation to Nixon, but they were shut out of the hosting hotel following pressure from the French government. We later met with Jean-Paul Sartre, who responded with an open letter supporting unconditional amnesty, which got some good visibility on both sides of the Atlantic.

Sartre echoed our slogan, amnesty for the future, "recognizing the citizen's right not to obey an unjust order, and further, not to participate in an imperialist war."

After our Paris conference was banned, I traveled with exile delegate Larry Svirchev to Rome, where we attended an inter-national anti-war conference and raised the amnesty issue. In Rome we met with good friends and allies. Although we had learned a hard lesson with Safe Return, we built solid ties with exiled war resisters in Europe, and forged an even stronger alliance with VVAW. These ties grew stronger in the years that followed.

The "abortive" international conference didn't make headlines in the U.S., but all our stateside supporters knew what had happened, and they were ready to get together and do something. Many were glad to know we had soured on Safe Return, since Safe Return had already alienated many others. Now our supporters wanted to put something together with Amex. With our solid alliance with VVAW, we felt ready to form a broader coalition. A series of meetings and conferences on both sides of the U.S.-Canada border in April and May of 1973 gave birth to the National Council for Universal Unconditional Amnesty (NCUUA).

So the campaign for amnesty expanded into a broad but still radical current in the anti-war movement. Walter and Virginia Collins sat on the NCUUA board to represent stateside draft resisters and parents of resisters, respectively. VVAW held a seat for bad paper vets. Jeanne Friedman, a strong supporter of anti-war activists living underground or in jail, held a seat for civilian resisters. I represented war resisters in exile. The Reverend Barry Lynn

Sartre on Amnesty

Amex editors met with philosopher Jean-Paul Sartre in Paris following the January 1973 peace accords.
He wrote this Open Letter on Amnesty.

I am writing to you from France. I know that the question of granting or not granting amnesty to deserters and draft resisters of the Vietnam war deeply divides your country. You may feel that this conflict is an internal matter concerning the United  States and thus does not regard Europeans.

However, since this problem is a sequel of a war waged for many years against a foreign country it seems to me that any foreign country has the right to give its viewpoint. As for me, in my capacity as President of the Russell Tribunal which found the American government guilty of numerous war crimes and of genocide in Vietnam, I shall try to convey the viewpoint of the majority of Europeans...

There are very nearly a million men concerned by amnesty: war resisters, deserters, persons having left the Army with less-than-honorable discharges. This is a far cry from the "few hundred" to whom your administration has at times scornfully referred. If we add to this figure the families of these men, it is clear that we are confronted with a deep rift that the Vietnam war has created in America.

The only just amnesty must be unconditional (no alternative service) and universal. This is a political problem. The intention is obviously not to demoralize the Army, but to recognize the citizen's right not to obey an unjust order, and further, not to participate in an imperialist war.

And we, the people of Europe, have the right to call for this amnesty as a sign that your government has no intention of someday involving us in an unjustifiable war.

Jean-Paul Sartre

Paris, France

February 1973

(published in Amex-Canada, March-April 1973,
and The New York Review of Books, April 19, 1973)

represented the National Council of Churches. He proved a strong ally: a member of our generation whom we found to be an honest, committed soldier of his faith. He judged us to be right and the government to be wrong. Aside from that he did not judge. Barry later led Americans United for Separation of Church and State, becoming a major force in opposition to rightist evangelism. Karl Bissinger represented the War Resisters League, and was an invaluable friend. He simply loved and gave unconditional support to resisters, whom he perceived to be living his beliefs. Henry Schwarzschild represented the ACLU Project on Amnesty, and was in some ways the "power behind the throne." Irma Zigas, an energetic leader of Women Strike for Peace as well as WRL, became NCUUA's executive director. She counted on Henry to turn the money spigot on and off as expedient.

As the exile representative on the NCUUA board, I worked closely with Irma from 1973 on, including a brief stint in the NCUUA office from August 1974 to the summer of 1975. (My charges of violating the draft law had been dismissed in spring 1972, so I was free to travel or live in the USA without legal concerns.) NCUUA was complicated and a bit lumpy politically. Some wanted a liberal solution, to be achieved through lobbying in Washington. We wanted nothing to do with Washington politicians. But this lobbying was essential politics for Schwarzschild and Zigas. We had to acknowledge that ultimately amnesty would come from Washington, though we wanted a massive public education campaign to justify total amnesty, since the war was wrong and it was right to resist.

For Amex and VVAW this caused much friction in the NCUUA councils, but we endured it with an eye to maintaining disciplined support for universal unconditional amnesty. Without our continued participation "amnesty" would have gotten watered down to some type of conditional amnesty or alternative service that would allow war resisters (or at least *some* of us) to "be forgiven" for our supposed crimes.

A Gold Star Mother, Louise Ransom, joined the NCUUA board in 1973. She and another Gold Star Mother, Pat Simon, devoted themselves tirelessly to the amnesty struggle. The "gold star" phrase signifies a parent who lost a son or daughter in war. As with active duty GIs and veterans, it would be hard for anyone to refute a Gold Star Mother who supported amnesty for war resisters. Patriotism is the key element in the Gold Star label, challenging anyone to feel anything but sympathy and solidarity with a mother's loss of a child. But patriotism was at the core of our dispute with the government: could we consider war criminal Nixon patriotic? Could an illegitimate war be considered patriotic? Many people thought so, which made the by-definition patriotism of a Gold Star mom irrefutable, even when she supported "traitorous" war resisters.

Years later, at the 1976 Democratic National Convention, Louise Ransom made a hugely important contribution by nominating war resister Fritz Efaw for vice president, in a stunningly dramatic appeal for amnesty. Disabled veteran Ron Kovic made the seconding speech, followed by Fritz. The impact was overpowering – not merely on the delegates and the TV audience but also on candidate Jimmy Carter. He committed himself to granting some type of amnesty, which was watered down a lot after he took office in January 1977.

All this took years of constant organizing to achieve.

When Nixon was re-elected by a landslide in 1972 against the anti-war candidate McGovern, many were despondent. But I bet my friend Jack Colhoun that Nixon would not make it through his term. I won the bet. The Watergate investigation showed that Nixon's "dirty tricks" were endless. We knew that. We also knew he would not survive the scandal. The pace of change was on our side. The tide of history was moving our way. It was exhilarating. We had an opening to say what we had to say, and find deep and wide support. So now we were the point of a lance of an international movement for amnesty.

Reflections:

My role as "exile representative" with NCUUA was challenging. I was like an "ambassador" in New York for the war resister exile community. I was pressured by NCUUA staff and board members on a daily basis to be more compromising. We had forged the coalition with its lengthy, cumbersome name to clarify our refusal to compromise. NCUUA staff wanted to lobby congressional representatives, which involved constant talk of compromise, while the Amex perspective was to wage a massive national education campaign to build support for "no compromise" on universal, unconditional amnesty. My efforts to make this happen were often at cross purposes with other NCUUA staff and board members. So there was frequent wrangling about time and resources, and an atmosphere of mutual suspicion.

The delicate art of cross-class coalition building is never easy. But I think it's necessary. In the late 1920s and early '30s, the left in Germany tended to dismiss the Social Democrats as "social fascists," with disastrous results. Later on alliances between left and middle forces allowed for breakthroughs against fascism. It's an important lesson for today.

Vietnam veterans mobilized in 1972 across the country.
Many of them forged an alliance with war resisters.

George Washington's famous comparison of "sunshine patriots" and "winter soldiers"[4] got an echo from the VVAW, who organized a series of high-visibility actions around this theme. They hammered away at Nixon as a sunshine patriot, and made it clear that their anti-war fight was the true expression of patriotism. This was a critically important message, since Nixon and all the other war makers have always made it seem the *only* patriotic stance was supporting their wars – uncritically, of course. We wholeheartedly supported VVAW's very successful Winter Soldier Investigation in Detroit in late 1973, an event that put the war criminals on trial by presenting testimony from dozens of vets. Then, in the spring of 1974 Amex helped VVAW get the NCUUA Steering Committee to endorse a July 4, 1974 VVAW demonstration in Washington that took the campaign to the streets. This demonstration had five demands: universal and unconditional amnesty; implement the Paris Peace Agreements and end all aid to the South Vietnamese puppet regime; a single-type discharge for all vets; decent benefits

---

[4] Thomas Paine originated the concept; Washington read Paine's pamphlet to soldiers at Valley Forge, to boost morale.

for all vets; and Kick Nixon Out. This last demand was coming true before our eyes. The Watergate scandal was blowing up in Nixon's face, and forced him to resign a month later in August 1974.

The Winter Soldier demonstration was exactly what Amex wanted. I was preparing to relocate to New York to take a staff position at NCUUA, and this demonstration served as a "pointer" to what I hoped to do. But like everything at the time, it was complicated by life changes. My intense level of activism had strained my relationship with Carol Woolverton, my Toronto partner since early 1970. She had left me and Toronto a few months earlier to live in Vancouver on Canada's west coast. As my plans developed I asked her to reconsider, and to go with me as I returned to the U.S. She agreed, so I travelled by train from Toronto to Vancouver to reunite with her. We then took a "drive-away" car from Vancouver to the San Francisco Bay Area, where we met with my parents and told them of our plans. (This wasn't a true "homecoming" as far as my parents were concerned, but they were very nice to Carol.) Then we hitched rides from Berkeley to Washington, stopping briefly in Reno, Nevada, to get married in a chapel there, as the most expedient way for Carol to legally join me in the U.S. (Some people said going to the chapel was riskier than going to the casinos in Reno!) We made it to Washington and joined the demonstration, and then returned to Toronto to pull our lives together for the move to New York.

Carol and I had barely finished our packing for the move when Nixon finally resigned to avoid impeachment on August 9, 1974. He was immediately pardoned as a first act by former Vice President Ford, who then tried to cover himself by extending "clemency" to draft resisters, but not to military resisters or militant anti-war activists. The stark contrast between Ford's "pardoning" Nixon and offering a punitive conditional clemency to draft resisters served to unify exiled war resisters in a boycott of the unjust program.

Amex convened the International Conference of Exiled American War Resisters in September 1974 in Toronto. Representatives from Sweden, France, and Great Britain joined others from across Canada. All united in the call for a boycott of the Ford clemency program. We got strong endorsements from our supporters in the U.S., plus a flood of positive media coverage. We knew the boycott by itself would not be enough. Two Amex leaders, Steve Grossman and Gerry Condon, agreed to undertake speaking tours in the U.S., gambling that we could generate enough visibility and support for them that U.S. authorities would not arrest them. It was a sign of the times: the tactic was successful. Steve was facing charges of draft resistance, and could have been seized and thrown in jail at any time. But he and his long-time partner Evangeline Mix toured numerous cities and college campuses in the Midwest, including an amnesty conference in Louisville, Kentucky. The results were massive positive publicity and a groundswell of support, after which they returned safely to Toronto.

Gerry's gamble was far riskier. He had already been convicted *in absentia* by an Army court martial for desertion after leaving Fort Bragg years earlier. So he already had a ten-year sentence hanging over his head. With all this in mind, we planned and prepared his return with great care. He and his partner Sandy Rutherford would "surface" in Washington, DC, as guests of honor at a large "Americans for Amnesty" conference, co-hosted by former Attorney General Ramsey Clark, and Gold Star Mother Louise Ransom. Getting them there was "half the fun." I had the job of coordinating their travel from Toronto to New York, where we met clandestinely in a Greenwich Village coffee house, Caffe Reggio. They then traveled by train to DC, to a tremendous reception and lots of live TV coverage. It was the kick-off of a national campaign. After the conference they flew to Los Angeles and conducted a non-stop West Coast speaking tour. In fact, Gerry just kept touring, and about nine months later he received a "bad conduct" discharge from the Army in the mail. My impression from then on was that Gerry's tour never really ended – he had transformed into a national organizer of anti-war veterans. He has been a leader of Veterans For Peace for years.

The boycott of the Ford Clemency program continued throughout 1974 and 1975. Its main success was to build stronger and stronger support for a true amnesty. However, a "loophole" opened which provided military resisters with a chance to resolve their situation. The Army brass were anxious to reduce the numbers of "non-performers" in the ranks. Stockades at bases across the country were jammed, with still more bitter and rebellious GIs returning from Asia, causing headaches under the brass hats. Anti-war GI counselors heard and spread the word that some bases were "expediting" the process of clearing the stockades. So some of our "long-term AWOLs" – GIs who were "absent without official leave" – could turn themselves into these bases, and be released with a less than honorable discharge in a matter of days. This was not the solution we were fighting for, but it was expedient, and a big relief for some resisters. We passed the word along while continuing the campaign for universal, unconditional amnesty, which included the demand for a single-type discharge for all veterans: the largest group with legal impediments caused by resistance to the war machine.

Towards the end of 1975, as the 1976 election cycle began, we mounted a campaign to make true amnesty a major issue. As a result of the clemency boycott and Steve and Gerry's speaking tours, support was strong nearly everywhere for our demands. NCUUA affiliates had sprung up as part of local churches and on college campuses. Amex prepared a campaign packet with sets of questions and answers for supporters to use in pressing candidates on the issue. Exile women became a significant factor, as a number of them fanned out across the country, working in coordination with local chapters of VVAW as well as with Clergy and Laity Concerned About the War in Vietnam. We also forged an alliance with the Indochina Peace and Friendship caravans that were touring the country to press the issues of a true amnesty and a just end to the U.S. war in Indochina. Gerry toured with Don Luce, a CALC leader who had been in Vietnam and witnessed the "tiger cages" that were used to torture members of the National Liberation Front captured by the South Vietnamese puppet government, under U.S. orders. They were a perfect combination, and garnered widespread support.

This organizing helped us influence delegates to the Democratic National Convention, slated for New York City in August of 1976. One of the resisters in England, Fritz Efaw, whom we had met in Paris in early 1973, got himself nominated as an alternate delegate to the convention. This situation provided a huge opportunity. Intensive and painstaking efforts led to huge results.

First, amnesty forces had to fight for Fritz to be allowed to attend the convention despite being an indicted draft resister. Then we had to build enough visibility on his arrival to keep him from being grabbed and swept far away from the convention. I was charged with media coordination, something I had developed a knack for over the years. So when Fritz arrived at Kennedy Airport, he was met by a huge press conference and a spirited crowd of supporters. Even though federal marshals did grab him, our volunteer attorneys managed to convince a federal magistrate in Brooklyn to let him attend the convention and deal with the charges afterwards. We then put together a solid core of seasoned amnesty movement organizers to work the convention. An Amex crew composed of Steve, Gerry and myself joined the NCUUA staff plus members of Clergy and Laity Concerned, the Greenwich Village Independent Democrats' amnesty committee, Gold Star Parents for Amnesty and several others. Together we set about proving what a small group of dedicated organizers can do.

The next task was to gather enough petition signatures in about 36 hours to call for a 20-minute discussion of amnesty in open convention debates. In about 36 hours we found 582 signers. That was more than enough, but the official Democrats chose to shut the initiative down. No problem. Gathering the signatures gave us momentum for the next step: working to get fifty delegate signatures to nominate Fritz for vice president. Convention heavies tried to stop us again, but we still got more than enough signatures. Then they told us Fritz was too young to be nominated. So our petition crew went out again, this time to get signatures to nominate Gold Star mother Louise Ransom, whose age met the constitutional requirement. At this point the Party leadership realized they had been out-maneuvered, and granted us fifteen minutes to nominate and second Efaw for Vice President.

Drawing on his rich experience in the theatre, Steve Gross-man proposed the political and emotional impact of having two resonant characters nominate and second Efaw for Vice President. First came Gold Star Mother Louise Ransom, then Vietnam veteran Ron Kovic, confined to a wheelchair due to paralysis from the chest down. The effect was stupendous.

"My credentials for addressing this convention have been earned in the hardest possible way," Louise Ransom told the delegates and the TV viewers. "My oldest son was killed in Vietnam on Mother's Day, 1968," she continued, as the crowd began to pay full attention. "The only way that we can give meaning to the lives of our sons and to guarantee that their deaths shall not have been for nothing is to demonstrate that we have learned something from them, and ensure that never again will there be another Vietnam. Total amnesty," she concluded, "would be a fitting memorial to the sacrifice of my son. Therefore, with pride, I put into nomination the name of exiled war resister Fritz Efaw." The crowd rose to its feet in applause, many with tears in their eyes.

When Ron Kovic was wheeled to the podium, the crowd fell silent. "I am the living death. Your Memorial Day on wheels. Your Yankee Doodle Dandy. Your John Wayne come home. Your Fourth of July firecracker exploding in the grave…." Kovic's words pierced the silence, cutting through the convention's bombastic rhetoric with some of the bitter truth of the Vietnam War. He told how his childhood patriotism was changed forever by his experience in Vietnam: accidentally killing one of his own men; shooting a group of innocent Vietnamese civilians, including two small children; and being shot himself and paralyzed for life. He spoke of enlisting in the Marines and going to Vietnam for two tours of duty, of turning against the war and later speaking out "wherever people would listen to me." He concluded, "I have the proud distinction of nominating Fritz Efaw for Vice President of the United States. Welcome home, Fritz!"

Then Fritz came to the podium and he and Ron Kovic embraced. "Welcome home, Fritz!" The words echoed through the hall and around the country. The delegates were on their feet, some cheering, others crying. Large amnesty banners wound through the crowd proclaiming "Universal Unconditional Amnesty," "Veterans Need Amnesty Too," and "Total Amnesty Now." Then Fritz spoke. He told the audience that the proposed draft resisters-only pardon would remove his own liability, but that he had "chosen to come home at the risk of imprisonment to tell you more about those Americans in jeopardy due to their opposition to the War, because we must ensure that all of them are included in next January's presidential pardon." After explaining, category-by-category, the various types of war resisters that needed amnesty, he concluded, "I am proud to come to this convention to represent war resisters. The risk involved in coming before you was certainly worth taking. I respectfully decline nomination for Vice President of the United States. I seek no office, and no further recognition." He received a standing ovation. He then made his way around the convention floor, pushing Ron Kovic's wheelchair, meeting and talking with the delegates.

That moment was NCUUA's greatest achievement in political theatre. A key lesson was that our movement did not need to read lines that someone else had written for us. The Vietnam War had produced enough tragedy and courage. All we needed was an audience willing to listen. The convention provided us with a stage. A dedicated core of amnesty activists, working day and night at the convention, injected some reality into an otherwise banal political celebration. But without similar tireless efforts by amnesty activists throughout the U.S., none of it would have been possible. (This report on the convention and its aftermath is adapted from the Amex Memoirs: https://cdm15932.contentdm.oclc.org/digital/collection/p15932coll8/id/9501)

The result of the convention was vastly increased visibility for the amnesty issue, but we still had lots of work to do. "Amnesty" still could be interpreted many different ways, and we knew candidate Carter would do his best to water it down. So we had to mobilize and educate as much as we could, and keep the pressure on. Amex believed the amnesty movement needed to focus on the dangers of class and race inequities of the Carter plan, and to explain why war resisters were right to resist the unjust U.S. war in Indochina.

Many liberal amnesty supporters wanted to give Carter "the benefit of the doubt," and settle for whatever he might give. Our hard core thought otherwise. The Carter organization had invited Amex to submit a position paper on amnesty before the convention. A "friendly" contact on the Carter staff counseled us to trust Carter, because once he was elected, his amnesty program would amount to "just about" what we wanted – though "it wouldn't look or sound like universal and unconditional amnesty." That was the tipoff. We had work to do, not only with the general public and the media, but also with Carter's inner circle. After having temporarily assigned a liberal ACLU lawyer from Texas to be his key adviser on amnesty, Carter then transferred the job to his long-time political associate Charles Kirbo, a conservative Georgian and a senior partner in one of the South's most powerful law firms.

NCUUA was able to arrange an amnesty delegation meeting with Kirbo. One of his main concerns was that if vets with bad papers had them upgraded to General or Honorable, they would be eligible for veterans' benefits. He also expressed worry that a Carter amnesty might jeopardize U.S. ability to raise a conscript army in the future. This, of course, was always one of our goals in the fight for amnesty. Our key message had always asserted the right to resist unjust wars of aggression. The meeting made it clear that lots more pressure would be needed.

From the night of the election in early November until Inauguration Day in late January, media attention regarding amnesty was intense, nearly all of it focused on Toronto. Amex was deluged with U.S., international, and Canadian media seeking amnesty interviews with exiled war resisters. In early December I took time off from my regular job in New York to go to Toronto for discussions with Jack Colhoun and Steve Grossman about how to increase the pressure on Carter.

I had been somewhat "out of the loop" since leaving the NCUUA staff in mid-1975 to get a regular job. (My participation with Amex and NCUUA staff at the Democratic convention was a kind of "cameo.") I had left the NCUUA staff after losing credentials as exile representative when I made the mistake of endorsing a Congressional lobbying initiative in the spring of 1975. It was a bitter lesson, but we tried to put it behind us at campaign "hot points" like the convention and the pre-inauguration sprint.

I proposed a massive border crossing by a crowd of exiled draft resisters and deserters, together with anti-war vets and civilians, to precede the pardon announcement and defy Washington to make arrests. I believed such a tactic would galvanize support for true amnesty, and generate wide media coverage, just as the boycott of Ford's clemency program had done. I suggested we include exiles from Sweden and France, even though it would add to the cost. Getting sufficient resources for such a bold move would be very difficult. After much discussion, we decided instead to try to host a major amnesty conference in Toronto that would respond to the Carter pardon. The conference would include exile representatives from Europe and other parts of Canada, veterans and NCUUA activists. Funding would still present a major problem, but we figured NCUUA could be persuaded to sponsor such an event, even if we had to get the process started on our own.

I volunteered to start a fundraising effort in New York, and Gerry and Sandy did the same in San Francisco. As part of his non-stop touring in early 1975, Gerry had launched Amnesty for Vets, a crucial initiative for the long-term. Amex agreed to provide seed money so Gerry and Sandy could raise more. Meanwhile Steve began talks with NCUUA staff to get the conference sponsored. The approach worked: take the initiative, get the ball rolling, and seek support. We announced the International Conference of War Resisters and Veterans for January 29-30, 1977, to be sponsored by NCUUA and hosted by Amex in Toronto. Amex took on the formidable task of pre-conference preparation by mobilizing numbers of Toronto exiles to help with the many responsibilities of hosting such a conference: security, day care, publicity, housing and logistics. The usual influx of hate mail, coupled with threats from the fascist Western Guard of Toronto (racist and anticommunist graffiti) alerted us to the need for serious security, especially with the Black vets we hoped to have at the conference, plus a featured speech by the President of the Union of Vietnamese in Canada.

Amex bolstered its leadership group with Gerry from San Francisco and myself from New York, plus numerous local supporters and early arrivals of exiles from Sweden, France and other parts of Canada. All of these people had several years of experience working on amnesty. Amex then gave a detailed political orientation to the expanded leadership group. Both Jack and Steve had placed significant articles on amnesty in *The Nation* and *The New York Times Magazine* just before the conference, which helped make their backgrounders and political analysis even more convincing to the new leadership group. Gerry Condon was able to bring a small delegation of veterans to the conference from San Francisco, and I invited my friends Terry Klug and John Catalinotto to come with me from New York. They had been lead organizers for the American Servicemen's Union (ASU), which published *The Bond* from 1967 to 1974 – a militant anti-war voice among GIs at bases across the country as well as in Vietnam. Terry's 17 months in the Fort Leavenworth stockade, and the fact that *The Bond* had reached tens of thousands of active duty GIs over the years gave them great credibility. Terry confided to me that he was very impressed with Steve's masterful job of chairing this important conference.

The conference timing was perfect: a week after the White House announcement of the Carter pardon on January 21, 1977, Carter's first full day in office. The media described the initial Amex response as "bitter disappointment" at Carter's unconditional pardon for draft resisters and non-registrants, which excluded military deserters or AWOLs, other veterans with less-than-honorable discharges, and civilians with anti-war charges or convictions. The administration promised a "special Pentagon study" to make recommendations concerning deserters and some bad paper vets.

Amex blasted the Carter pardon as thoroughly discriminatory on the basis of class and race, for including mainly white, middle class draft resisters, but excluding poor white and minority forms of war resistance. The pardon seemed like a trick. Apparently Carter didn't feel secure enough politically to deal with military deserters, and was stalling for time to arrange some sort of negotiated decision. This "half a loaf" pardon vindicated the Amex decision to host a conference in Toronto and make an appropriate response. Some liberal amnesty supporters were offering "conditional praise" for the pardon, and NCUUA staff director Irma Zigas had the gall to criticize Amex for its hard line. But in the course of a telephone conference call, the liberals withdrew their lukewarm support of the pardon. As people supporting this tendency were to learn at the Toronto conference, it could be difficult to praise the Carter pardon in front of a deserter or bad paper vet!

The conference itself reflected careful planning by the expanded exile leadership group, and negotiation with NCUUA staff and liberal supporters. Steve Grossman co-chaired with NCUUA staff leader Irma Zigas. Jack Colhoun and Gerry Condon – both military deserters – spoke on behalf of Amex, together with draft resister Joe Jones and civilian anti-war activist Bruce Beyer. These were people I knew well: I first met Gerry in 1965 at the University of San Francisco; and I had helped Bruce get to Sweden in 1969. Both of them knew most of the delegations from Sweden and France, who issued a ten-minute joint statement. Bob Chenoweth, an anti-war former U.S. prisoner of war, also spoke, as did the president of the Union of Vietnamese in Canada, Vinh Sinh. The opening session of the conference also featured Gold Star mothers Louise Ransom and Pat Simon, and Carolyn Minugh, mother of Dave Minugh, an exile delegate from Sweden. A conference steering committee, including all the regular NCUUA Steering Committee members, plus representatives of the exile constituencies and veterans, were responsible for conducting the conference and drafting resolutions.

This careful preparation gave good results: the opening day of the conference was clearly under the leadership of Amex and its allies. As the first day ended, the NCUUA staff and other liberals tried to take control of the political direction and soften the tone and politics of the conference resolutions and public statements. One of that group even had the nerve to draft a "collective letter" to the new government of postwar Vietnam accusing it of political repression. Drafting committees stayed up until dawn wrangling over both political essence and tone. In the end, both sides were satisfied that if we did not get all we wanted, we got what we needed. And there was no criticism of the new Vietnamese government, a stance with which the conference majority exhibited deep solidarity.

The conference resolutions and decisions concretized NCUUA's political obligation to deserters, bad paper vets, and civilian anti-war protesters either "wanted" or with "criminal" records. We made it clear that the amnesty fight could not stop when only white and middle class draft resisters had been pardoned but others – the majority of those needing amnesty – were excluded. It was a tough argument, since the liberals felt they were done. In fact they really *were* done, and hoped to end their commitment to the amnesty struggle then and there, or as soon as possible. But the conference delegates closest to Amex made a clear commitment to continue the fight and win justice for military resisters and vets. That effort would become a slogging battle, and a story of its own.

UP AGAINST THE
BULKHEAD

THIS PAPER CANNOT LEGALLY BE TAKEN FROM YOU, ACCORDING TO DOD DIRECTIVE 1325.6 "POSSESSION OF UNAUTHORIZED MATERIAL MAY NOT BE PROHIBITED."

98 Clancy Street, San Francisco, California 94134   Issue 13   January 1973   Free to GIs

MILITARY REVOLTING!

At the same time many Americans feel powerless to change the course of Nixon's ship of state a hundred and thirty-five sailors forced a United States aircraft carrier to turn around dead in its tracks and return from sea duty to its port in San Diego.

The 150 had staged a sit-down strike in the mess deck of the attack carrier USS Constellation. They settled in for a long stay, and remained calm, disciplined and unified in the face of everything from sweet-talking Human Relations counselors to a riot squad toting loaded M-16s with fixed bayonets. Unable to feed the rest of the ship's 4000 men, and unable to split up the group Captain Ward was forced to turn "his" ship around in order to get "the problem" off the boat.

But even when the 150 were on the pier and off the boat they remained a problem to Capt. Ward. They stuck together and refused to get back on until their demands for fair and equal treatment by the ship's command were dealt with. Again, they sit down together, refused to work, and disobeyed a direct order to get back on the boat. See the full story on page four.

VIETNAM	PHILIPPINES	BILLY DEAN SMITH
What Lies Behind the Peace Talk? How Will It Affect You? See Page 8.	When Martial Law Was Declared, American Friends of the GI Movement Were Jailed & Deported. Interview on Page 3.	Acquitted of Fragging Charges At Fort Ord, California See Page 15.

Active duty soldiers and sailors rebelled at bases across the country and around the world. This resulted in half a million "less-than-honorable" discharges – a life sentence to discrimination.

One of the slogans of the Toronto conference was "On to Washington!" During the first ten days of February, the amnesty movement actually did move on to Washington for a series of veteran-oriented amnesty actions, and an "Appeal for Reconciliation" conference sponsored by the American Friends Service Committee (AFSC). A veterans' vigil picket line marched in front of the Veterans Administration building, and on February 5, 1977, a spirited rally of several hundred demonstrated in Lafayette Park in front of the White House. A delegation of recently-pardoned draft resisters and other

Amex people traveled from Toronto to highlight exile support for bad paper vets. And the Appeal for Reconciliation Conference sparked a lot of media coverage for amnesty and the demands for U.S. recognition of Vietnam and reconstruction aid. About 80,000 signatures from the Appeal petition campaign were delivered to the White House.

It took the new Carter Administration more than two months to keep its promise to provide a program for deserters and veterans with less-than-honorable discharges. On April 5, the Pentagon announced that Vietnam-era deserters with no other military charges pending against them would be eligible to return to military control for expedited less-than-honorable discharges. They could then apply, along with about 432,000 vets with general and undesirable discharges, to have their bad papers reviewed under a Special Discharge Review Program (SDRP). Better than nothing, this program mainly served the Pentagon's purposes: weeding out undesirable personnel and reducing pressure on the stockades and courts martial. It was meant to be quiet. Carter and the Pentagon wanted as little publicity for it as possible, and to set it to expire six months later, in October 1977.

That meant the amnesty movement and GI organizers and counselors would need to spread the word as aggressively as possible, while continuing to press for real justice for bad paper vets. This became the job for a reconstituted amnesty coalition, largely focused on and led by Vietnam era veterans. While Amex continued to wrangle with NCUUA staff coordinators over whether and how NCUUA might continue the fight, I became involved in a New York-based organizing effort called the Military and Veterans Action Committee (MVAC) – hoping to emulate Gerry Condon's effective "Amnesty for Vets" effort. I also helped recruit a new NCUUA staff coordinator. Barbara Webster had worked for some years on the staff of the People's Coalition for Peace and Justice, the national anti-war coalition. Barbara gave me hope that a reconstituted NCUUA might keep on keepin' on for vets and deserters, at least through October 1977. But the transition was difficult, with lots of internal wrangling. It was really thanks to the solid support of Karl Bissinger of War Resisters League, Duane Shank of the National Interreligious Board for Conscientious Objectors and NCUUA staffer Susan Ikenberry, together with Amex people, that we were able to sustain commitment for amnesty work.

But it was difficult. Amex, "running on empty," felt compelled to delve deeply into details of the Pentagon's lumpy and inconsistent program for deserters. This was important, because the clock was ticking, and lots of deserters in Canada needed detailed information so they could take the next step in their lives. By this time many of them were married with new families. They also had to deal with the mixed feelings of their families "back home." The various branches of the U.S. military and all the different base commands added to the complexity with their various interpretations of the new program. Marine commanders at Camp Pendleton, for example, made it clear they would slam any returning AWOLs in the brig and start court martial proceedings. Variations on this theme happened at other bases. Jack Colhoun and Joe Somsky managed to establish a "hot line" to a White House staffer, but attempts to iron out these wrinkles met with limited success.

Meanwhile Gerry and I continued with our vets and GI work. The new NCUUA staff organized a "New Directions" conference for June in Milwaukee, to maximize outreach efforts to vets while clarifying the political thrust of the re-constituted amnesty movement, with focus on the legal and political meaning of the two steps of the Carter pardon program. There was a workshop on "Lessons of Vietnam and Future Wars," and a panel on the role of women in the amnesty movement. The assembly decided that NCUUA would continue to publicize and criticize the Carter second-step pardon, emphasizing the demand for a single-type discharge. It also decided to begin work on military and counter-recruitment in high schools and elsewhere, to support GI organizing struggles, and to continue work on civilian anti-war resister issues, following up the slogan developed by the left earlier in the year at the Toronto conference: "Amnesty for the Future, Not Just the Past." This slogan had been a favorite of mine, highlighting our key goal: to make it harder for the U.S. government to get more cannon fodder for its unjust wars of aggression around the world.

The conference also called for all such work to advance the fight against sexism and racism. It highlighted the important contributions made by women to the anti-war and amnesty movement, giving more visibility to women war resisters. It concretized an anti-racist program, committing to continued work around bad paper vets – disproportionately from minority communities – and to supporting the Camp Pendleton Fourteen case (fourteen Black Marines who resisted attacks by the Ku Klux Klan within the Marine Corps and now faced long stockade sentences).

This determined effort to deliver the results of the amnesty campaign to deserters and bad paper vets produced significant results. By October 1977, thousands of military resisters (AWOLs and others) were able to get some relief and get on with their lives. It was frustrating not to win everything we had fought for over so many years, but we assessed that we had indeed won major political victories. Here is a summary from the Amex memoirs:

During our six-year amnesty struggle, Amex was involved in surfacing a military deserter at the 1972 Democratic National Convention, whose arrest brought the amnesty question to the floor of the convention hall. In 1976, we helped win fifteen minutes of prime time TV to nominate a draft resister for vice president. We battled three presidents – Richard Nixon, Gerald Ford, and Jimmy Carter – over the amnesty issue. We saw Nixon resign in disgrace after he had called us criminals. After pardoning Nixon, when Ford offered a punitive "clemency" program, we called a highly successful boycott. During the 1976 election campaign, we helped develop a grassroots amnesty coalition which made amnesty a hot issue.

From the time of Carter's nomination in July 1976 until his inauguration in January 1977, we led the attack against the class and race discrimination of Carter's proposed draft resister-only pardon. After Carter announced his unconditional pardon on January 21, 1977, we hosted an international amnesty conference that blasted Carter for not including deserters, bad paper vets, or civilians with anti-war charges and records. On April 5, 1977, the Carter Administration announced the details of its program for some deserters and limited categories of vets with less-than-honorable discharges. Amex led NCUUA in attacking the inadequacy of the program, while working hard to make it accessible to as many deserters and vets as possible.

In 1971, at the beginning of Amex's struggle for amnesty, both supporters and critics often told us there would never be an unconditional amnesty. At some point after the Vietnam War ended, it became likely that there would be some form of limited pardon. We believed it would benefit white, middle-class draft resisters at the expense of working class and minority war resisters. If the possibility of winning a broad unconditional amnesty existed, we believed it would require a widespread grassroots political campaign. We were determined to build such a grassroots movement, to force such a presidential action. Six years of struggle gave us many political victories, even though we didn't win our goal of universal and unconditional amnesty.

During the course of our political work in exile, we helped forge a new anti-war alternative: going into exile. From exile we were able to lead a popular movement through which we explained to the American people the reasons for our resistance and our amnesty demand. We helped to maintain the amnesty discussion for six years, and the popular debate about the

Vietnam War for two years after the liberation of Vietnam, and more than four years after the signing of the Paris Ceasefire Agreement.

All of this also changed our lives for the better. For many of us the decision to leave our country involved great risk. But life in exile was a huge learning experience. We can only be grateful to the millions of Canadians who made us feel welcome, and applied pressure to their government so Canada could be more of "a refuge from militarism." The Swedish government of the time went even further, basically providing a safe refuge for U.S. military deserters.

In my own case, the experience not only radicalized me, but provided an opportunity to develop skills and knowledge as a revolutionary organizer, which ultimately determined the direction for the rest of my life. It's true that there were sacrifices. I was over thirty when our amnesty campaign ended. It took most of another decade for me to "settle down" to a more-or-less-normal life style.

"More or less," for me, meant dedicating myself first to the endless task of stopping the U.S. war machine and fighting for a better world. Forty years later I haven't stopped, and hope I can continue indefinitely. But now I see the task is larger. Now it's clear we need a revolution. And while the odds seem long at the moment – after roughly four decades of reaction – I remain optimistic and confident. We're living in a breakthrough moment. We just need to seize the time, get organized, and fight to win!

The last slogan of our fight for total amnesty was "Amnesty for the Future – Not Just the Past!" It's even more relevant today than it was in 1977. I believe the only way veterans can get justice will be if the *mission and essence* of the U.S. war machine are forced to change. The war machine is the instrument for establishing and maintaining U.S. domination across the globe. Its mission is to force the countries and peoples dominated by U.S. imperialism to submit to that domination.

When a people's movement is strong enough to stop the U.S. war machine, the veterans will get justice, and the repressive and punitive system that has always been used to force workers in uniform to obey unjust orders will be dismantled. It is most likely to happen from within, just as it did during the U.S. war in Vietnam. Soldiers will refuse to fight. They'll organize for their rights as citizens and humans. They'll be inspired by a liberation movement at home, as well as by the bravery and righteousness of their supposed "enemies." When this happens, it will usher in a new future – the future we're fighting for.

9 - *Supporting Revolutions Abroad and at Home!*

On April 30, 1975, when I got the news that Vietnam's national liberation forces had marched triumphantly into Saigon, kicking out the U.S. puppet government and causing the U.S. embassy staff to flee in helicopters, I bought a bottle of champagne and took it to the office of the War Resisters League to celebrate. The WRL office, at the corner of Bleecker and Lafayette Streets in Greenwich Village, hosted a variety of radical and progressive groups, including the National Council for Universal Unconditional Amnesty (NCUUA), where I had worked since August 1974, coordinating the war resister boycott of the Ford clemency program.

Not everyone celebrated with me. As a leftist I was part of a distinct minority in the anti-war movement. That didn't bother me much – liberal anti-communism prevailed among most anti-war people at that time, which I considered natural, given the constant blast of anti-communism in the U.S. political culture. But victory in Vietnam surely would prove to be a turning point. I figured it would stimulate more revolutions across the globe, and unleash victory parties and new revolutionary optimism, even in the heart of imperialism.[5]

I was partly right. In Africa, even before Vietnam's victory, popular forces were surging in Portugal's colonies of Mozambique, Guinea-Bissau, Cabo Verde and Angola. Portugal's colonial army cracked under the pressure, thus ending five centuries of colonial rule by the first European country to invade Africa, and unleashing a revolutionary tide on the western tip of the European continent. What started in Portugal as an anti-fascist uprising in April 1974, led by the Armed Forces Movement, became a massive popular movement for socialism. Farmers and factory workers who had quietly endured repression for decades, surged into the streets. They joined communist and socialist forces that had worked "underground" for more

---

[5] It may seem odd to consider "the fall of Saigon" as a victory. But it definitely was, after 30-plus years of non-stop fighting, led by the legendary Vietnamese leader, Ho Chi Minh. A benefit of living outside the USA for six years was an ability to see the world more objectively. Ho Chi Minh became my hero in the sixties, because of his selfless and steadfast patriotism – a stark contrast to the pseudo variety of Richard Nixon, whose "leadership" qualities ranged from bald-faced lies to brutal repression and global terrorism.

than two generations, and emerged to take over factories, march in the streets, and push the democratic military officers in the government to the left.

Across western Europe, the excitement was palpable. Many people hoped and dreamed that the anti-fascist surge would spread to the neighboring Spanish state, toppling the fascist regime of Generalissimo Franco, who had suppressed the Republican left in the Spanish Civil War of 1936-39, with help from Nazi Germany and fascist Italy. A revolution in Portugal had the potential to unleash revolutions across the continent.

I had to see it for myself. My wife Carol and I were part of a small Marxist study circle which turned its attention to these new developments. We decided to travel to Portugal as "red tourists." We landed in Lisbon in September 1975, just in time to join gigantic street marches and rallies in support of leftist leaders in the military government who were resisting a rightwing takeover. We witnessed close-up a battle between left and right, seeing the new U.S. ambassador Frank Carlucci play a significant role in bolstering the rightist side.

In 1961 Carlucci had been in the Congo as second secretary in the U.S. embassy (and a covert CIA agent). He was rumored to have masterminded the assassination of Patrice Lumumba, the new president of the Congo, which had just won independence after several centuries of colonial exploitation by Belgium. Carlucci went on to become Deputy Director of the CIA from 1978 to 1981, then Deputy Secretary of Defense from 1981 to '83, then Ronald Reagan's National Security Adviser from 1986 to '87, and finally Secretary of Defense to the end of Reagan's administration. After that he became chairman of the super-elite Carlyle Group, serving the interests of George H.W. Bush and associates. As a board member of the Rand Corporation (the Pentagon's number one think tank), he became founding co-chair of Rand's Center for Middle East Public Policy. Carlucci's list of credentials underscores the importance the U.S. elite attached to events in Portugal and in Portugal's former African colonies. He skillfully backed Portugal's rightist forces and prevented a successful revolution there. (Obituaries in the Washington Post and New York Times in mid-2018 lauded him as "a daredevil diplomat" who was also "cool, experienced and knowledgeable" – a perfect combination of talents.)

Meanwhile Angola, the largest and richest of Portugal's former colonies, became the next battleground due to enormous oil reserves and strategic position – bordering the Congo on the north and Namibia (Southwest Africa) on the south. Angola's independence would present a huge threat to apartheid South Africa (the most important U.S. ally in Africa at the time), as well as to western oil companies and their client governments. So Angola became a cold war hot spot, and a focal point of political confusion in the wake of the split on the left between the Soviet Union and China.

Angola's anti-colonial movement had been led for decades by the Popular Movement for the Liberation of Angola (MPLA), whose legendary leader, Agostino Neto, launched the liberation war against Portugal in 1961, with backing from the Soviet Union. After the Sino-Soviet split, Mao's China threw its support behind an upstart competing group, the National Liberation Front of Angola (FNLA), while the U.S. CIA backed another group, the National Union for the Total Independence of Angola (UNITA). This was a very low point for China's so-called "three worlds" policy.

Neither of these two competing groups had any importance of their own, and they were easily overcome as MPLA launched an attack on Luanda, the colonial capital, and then took over the government in November 1975. But the U.S. CIA, together with the South African government, helped UNITA and FNLA to regroup and fight again. The resulting civil war pitted these puppet forces against the MPLA government. U.S. and South African backing gave them staying power. The MPLA government appealed for help from revolutionary Cuba, which sent 25,000 troops to join in the fight. This support proved decisive, but the war dragged on for 13 years, until the MPLA and Cuban forces won a key battle that pushed the South African troops out and caused the U.S. puppet forces to surrender.[6]

While all this took place in Africa, the situation sparked major debates on the left in the USA, and helped me choose sides in the stormy political battles of the tiny U.S. left. In November 1975 I joined a march in defense of the MPLA. This event led me to Workers World Party, the march's main organizer. I had already read the polemics of "new communist" groupings who opposed MPLA and denounced its Soviet backers, as well as Cuba's military intervention. Even though I had earlier viewed Mao and China as "more revolutionary" than the USSR, it was easy to see that the U.S. government was waging proxy war against the USSR and Cuba in Angola, in

---

[6] Cuban forces, sent to fight in solidarity with the MPLA and African liberation, were generally described as "Soviet proxies" by the U.S. media. Fidel Castro said most Cubans have African blood in their veins, a legacy of centuries of colonialism and slavery, and could feel solidarity with Angola for themselves. A friend of mine is named Luanda, after the Angolan capital where she was born (where her father, a medical doctor from the Dominican Republic, was working during this period).

addition to suppressing Africa's anti-colonial revolution. This helped me understand that whatever shortcomings there might be in the Soviet Union, it was still the main source of support for anti-colonial revolution in Africa, as it had been in Vietnam. The logic struck me as simple: enemies of the U.S. empire were the good guys. And I wanted to support these forces against imperialism. This type of logic is easy to understand once the blinders imposed by the anti-communist U.S. media monopoly are removed.

Another significant factor that brought me to Workers World Party (WWP) was the American Servicemen's Union (ASU), led by Andy Stapp. Andy and the ASU were well known to politically active war resisters in Canada as one of the most effective forces in the GI resistance movement. If WWP backed the ASU, that made it attractive to me. But involvement didn't happen immediately. I had obligations to the amnesty movement that kept me very busy. In late 1976, about a year after the MPLA solidarity march, I showed up at a WWP meeting with hopes of finding support for the big amnesty conference planned for Toronto during the time of Carter's inauguration in January. Terry Klug and John Catalinotto – both of them leading ASU organizers – agreed to go to Toronto with me. After that we worked together non-stop. In July 1977, in the midst of an electrical blackout in New York City, I applied to join the party.

Joining is a process. You start as a candidate member. While you learn the ropes and come to understand the commitment, you are evaluated by the party. My friend Terry told me "you should expect to be carried out" – that is, after a lifetime in the struggle. Average age was difficult to gauge. At that time I was 30 – slightly younger than the average.

Although the party itself was founded in 1959, four of the five founding members had been active reds for more than two decades, going back to the Great Depression of the 1930s and the World War II period. The chairman, Sam Marcy, could trace his own red activism back to the 1920s. He once recalled that he and his brother first encountered the Soviet Red Army in their native Ukraine in 1918. His brother told him, "These guys are ours. Want to know how you can tell? Go ask one of them for a cigarette." Sam was too young to smoke, but he did it, and was convinced. He was an active communist from then on. As a hardline Leninist, he was won over to the left opposition in 1928, as Stalin consolidated power with purges. In the USA, this proved a fateful move. The U.S. Communist Party was surging forth in massive union drives and civil rights campaigns, growing rapidly to tens of thousands of members across the country. Sam was always an unusual left oppositionist – he defended the Soviet Union to his dying day, and likewise championed the revolutionary proletarian character of the Chinese revolution of 1949. He led a group of workers and intellectuals in Buffalo, NY, who finally emerged as Workers World Party following the triumph of the Cuban Revolution in 1959. The Cuban victory, and the burgeoning civil rights movement made the founders optimistic that a new wave of revolutionary possibilities lay on the horizon.

The post-WW2 anti-communist witch hunt was nearly over by 1959. Richard Nixon, Eisenhower's vice president and a key player in the witch hunt, was planning to run for president in 1960, but people were tired of him. After eight years as Vice President under Eisenhower – acting as a virtual partner of Senator Joe McCarthy in the endless Congressional hearings that caused anti-communist purges of numerous unions and generated a prevailing terror – his credibility was low. That was one meaning of "the torch has passed" in Jack Kennedy's inaugural speech. Especially among young people, but also the case for many others, there was a feeling that the stifling rightist atmosphere needed to end. Kennedy sought to manifest change with symbolism, like establishing the Peace Corps and offering a more-or-less-friendly reception to Martin Luther King, Jr. – actions not to be confused with substantial change. The opening that Kennedy perceived was also apparent to Sam Marcy, who had very substantial changes on his agenda.

The new party quickly took sides with revolutionary China in the early stages of the Sino-Soviet split. The point was to opt for world revolution rather than "peaceful coexistence," *a la* Krushchev. An early headline in Workers World newspaper said "Hail the Communes!" – a wholehearted endorsement of China's revolutionary direction. Next Workers World and its youth group, Youth Against War and Fascism (YAWF) became the first in the USA to hit the streets in support of the Vietnamese National Liberation Front. Workers World also actively defended armed Black resistance in the U.S. South by providing unconditional support for Robert F. Williams, the NAACP chapter leader in Monroe, North Carolina, who wrote *Negroes with Guns*. Later WWP became a strong defender of the Black Panther Party, once again showing unconditional support for Black liberation.

In 1974 WWP mobilized against a wave of racist reaction in Boston. People in white neighborhoods were violently obstructing buses that transported Black children to schools in white neighborhoods as part of court-ordered desegregation of the schools. The Ku Klux Klan had also mobilized, but *in support* of the white racists. WWP called for a National

March Against Racism in Boston that brought 25,000 people into the streets, pushed back the Klan, and changed the balance of forces. It followed up this victory by organizing a union for bus drivers, modeling a new type of union that depended on community support – and got it despite the racists in South Boston, who turned out to have more bark than bite. The bus driver union has become a force not only in Boston but throughout the country. Its leadership, a coalition of WWP leaders who work as bus drivers and rank-and-file union members, has won numerous battles – not only for decent contracts, but also in defense of the principle of busing and equality in education. It has also fought and won battles against old-fashioned red-baiting designed to destroy the union. A substantial percentage of the drivers in the union are Haitian, so the union is a major force against anti-immigrant hysteria in Boston. It's the kind of union that shows why socialists and communists should be union leaders!

When I joined the party during New York's electrical blackout of July 1977, the big issue was massive police repression of "looting," which the party described as a rebellion. With the streets dark and blocked, young people broke into stores and carted off food and groceries, electronics, and anything else they could carry. New York is a highly segregated city, so the battles were largely between Black and Latinx youth and white cops. Thousands of young people were arrested and taken to "The Tombs" (Manhattan House of Detention, near City Hall) – an aptly named jail where the youth were packed in while awaiting arraignment and trial. The party set up a picket line outside demanding the youth be released without charges. I was impressed with the tactic's boldness, which motivated me to sign up right away. For me it was an example of unconditional support for oppressed people, the significance of which might not be apparent at a given moment, but over time – that is, over the many times such support could be mobilized – it would have a significant effect. For example, during the rebellion at the notorious Attica prison in upstate New York in August 1971, Workers World's Prison Solidarity Committee was invited by the prisoners to send a representative to negotiate on their behalf, along with former Attorney General Ramsey Clark.

The U.S. prison system is a pillar of institutional racism in the USA, which leads the world in the percentage of its population behind bars. The total number of people in state, federal and local jails, or on parole, is by far the largest in the world – approximately equal to the combined total for "authoritarian" China and the Russian Federation.[7] The prison-industrial complex is a glaring continuation of the slave system, a stark reminder that the U.S. power system is dedicated to excluding and holding down people of color, especially African-Americans.[8]

The numbers of imprisoned African-American people far exceeds their numbers in higher education, and the cost per prisoner is much higher than the cost per pupil in the public universities. Judges could save billions of dollars in public funds by sentencing "offenders" to four years of university education at the institution of their choice, plus a stipend for living expenses, instead of sending them to the country's hell holes. Many of these concentration camps now have become profit centers, with prisoners' super-sub-minimum-wage labor sold to the highest bidder. The overall cost to the public is still a huge loss – even without factoring in the enormous costs of local police forces, the monstrous judicial system, or the extensive social costs of millions of wasted lives.

If there were fair access to jobs and other opportunities to meaningfully participate in society for the excluded people of color, the so-called "crime" rate would diminish to a vanishing point. But the systematic exclusion and discrimination against people of color is a basic element in the divide-and-rule strategy used by the capitalist system to hold the entire working class down.

Add to these outrages the current anti-immigrant hysteria, unleashed by President #45. I wrote recently about this:

The current horrors and scandals of Trump's cruelty and racism toward immigrants have made it easier for many to see some deeper realities. "Immigrants" from Europe in past centuries invaded the Americas in the name of "God" and their favorite national identity, then "justified" their slaughter and genocide of the people who lived here as a "manifest destiny" to take over and rule the Americas, either by killing off or "civilizing" those who

---

[7] www.prisonstudies.org/highest-to-lowest/prison-population-total. Parolees are not included in these comparisons. According to the US Bureau of Justice Statistics (BJS), 2.2 million adults were incarcerated in US federal and state prisons, and county jails in 2013 – about 1 in 110 of the U.S. resident population. Another 4.75 mil-lion adults (1 in 51) were on probation or on parole in 2013.

[8] See *The New Jim Crow: Mass Incarceration in the Age of Color-Blindness*, by Michelle Alexander. Also note the 13th Amendment: "Neither slavery nor involuntary servitude, *except as a punishment for a crime…*, shall exist within the United States…" *(Italics added.)*

stood in their way. The so-called "Indians" – indigenous peoples who occupied this land for millennia – lost essentially everything.

A recent New Yorker article by Masha Gessen offers a refreshing admission: "Now seems like a good moment to admit that we don't know what we are talking about when it comes to immigration." The article says, "The Trump Administration has succeeded in framing the debate as one between supporters of enforcing immigration law and supporters of open borders." Arch-racist Jeff Sessions is quoted: "I don't think there is a scriptural basis that justifies any idea that we must have open borders in the world today." The article goes on to say "Trump declared 'The Democrats want open borders.' Sadly, this is not true: no voice audible in the American political mainstream is making the argument for open borders."

Socialists make that argument. We say "there are no borders in the workers' struggle!" *(En la lucha obrera no hay frontera!)* We answer the "Christian" KuKluxer Sessions that we don't need a "scriptural" justification for open borders. Imperialism did it for us. It was imperialism that blasted open all the borders in all the countries in the world. Old fashioned "gunboat diplomacy," *a la* Teddy Roosevelt (who was fond of saying "speak softly but carry a big stick"), assured that American commerce, American values (*ie,* dollars), and American norms would be both "welcome" and dominant in all countries, first and foremost in those of "our America." There really have been no borders that had to be respected by U.S. imperialism. That remains true today. (An exception that proves the rule is the artificial 38th parallel "border" separating North and South Korea, imposed by the U.S. military in 1953, and defended today by one of the largest U.S. occupation forces in the world.)

Many people have been hurt by imperialism's open borders. Recently millions have had to abandon their homes and their countries for dear life in the wake of U.S. wars of "regime change" in Libya, Sudan, Syria, Yemen, Afghanistan and Somalia. In Latin America, over the last century, the U.S. imperialist "open borders" policy has caused millions of refugees of all types to flee their own countries. Endless violence and insecurity – all of it caused by imperialist domination – has forced people to flee for their own survival. In the case of Mexicans in the southwestern United States, many were either staying in or fleeing to land that historically was theirs. That's a major reason that Trump and his followers are so hysterical about terrorizing them and driving them out.

Refugees and migrants of all types go to the source of their problem: the USA or the western European imperialist countries, where the profits from their countries' exploitation have generated prosperity. But imperialist prosperity is waning and fading. Rich countries could in past decades absorb a lot of their former colonials. But their economies are shaky now. So the search for scapegoats and victims has intensified. In all the imperialist countries, the migrants and refugees of imperialist pillage and war are now being excluded, or rounded up and driven out. So it is in the USA, and Trump has cheered on his "populist" buddies to do the same in Europe.

What is this about? It's really about the decline of empire, accompanied by a frantic effort to blame it all on the refugees and migrants. When viewed in this light, Trump's vicious and racist attacks on immigrants and refugees are no less brutal and criminal. But they can be seen more objectively for what they are: one more manifestation of the demise of a dying system. The tasks of anti-imperialists remain the same – to defend the victims and scapegoats, and to do whatever we can to hasten this murderous system's demise.

In the meantime my wife and I have helped undocumented people fight deportation, together with many of our friends and thousands of other socialists.

In recent years I have realized that the battle for socialism must be much broader than WWP could mobilize from its isolated position on the far left. So I joined the Democratic Socialists of America (DSA), which together with Bernie Sanders have stimulated a much larger movement for socialism.

10 – Nicaragüita

Nicaraguan Sandinistas shot down a CIA cargo plane loaded with "70 Soviet-made AK-47 rifles and 100,000 rounds of ammunition, rocket grenades and other supplies" for the contras, in October 1986. It was piloted by Eugene Hasenfus, a former Marine who flew CIA supply missions during the Vietnam War. Hasenfus would later tell his Nicaraguan captors that he had flown more than ten such missions.

The Sandinistas posted a billboard *(inset)* with this message:
"More than a battalion of yours, blond invader,
will bite the dust in our rugged mountains."

I noticed the billboard when I first came to Nicaragua in 1987.

A Love Song to Nicaragua

Ay Nicaragua, Nicaragüita
La flor mas linda de mi querer
Abonada con la bendita,
Nicaragüita, sangre de Diriangen
Ay Nicaragua, sos mas dulcita
Que la mielita de tamagas,
Pero ahora que ya sos libre
Nicaragüita, yo te quiero mucho mas!
Pero ahora que ya sos libre
Nicaragüita, yo te quiero mucho mas!

Oh Nicaragua, little Nicaragua,
The most beautiful flower of my love
Blossomed with the blessing,
Little Nicaragua, blood of Diriangen
Oh Nicaragua, you're sweeter
Than the honey flower of tamagas,
But now that you're free
I love you even more!
– Luis Enrique Mejia Godoy,
Nicaraguan revolutionary troubadour

The Sandinista National Liberation Front toppled the U.S.-backed Somoza dictatorship in 1979 after a fierce guerrilla war that lasted more than a decade. They immediately instituted a massive land reform program, distributing most of the country's land to poor peasants after taking over the property of the Somoza family and its supporters. In 1980 the Sandinistas launched a literacy campaign, sending more than 100,000 teachers across the country to develop basic literacy for the whole population, both adults and children, winning the UNESCO Literacy award. The country's illiteracy rate dropped from over 50 percent to under 12 percent in the campaign's first year.

UNESCO also recognized Nicaragua's "exceptional health progress" under the Sandinistas. Average life expectancy in 1961, when the FSLN was founded, was 48 years; it rose to 60 by 1984, after five years of revolution; by 2016 it was 75. Before 1979 more than 90 percent of health resources went to just ten percent of the population. The Sandinistas established a free national health service available to all Nicaraguans. They launched a "health *brigadista*" program with Sandinista youth to provide basic health education across the country. They built hundreds of new primary healthcare facilities and trained thousands of new health professionals, with help from a corps of Cuban doctors.

Other achievements of the revolution included improved rural and urban working conditions; free unionization for all workers; price controls for basic commodities; improved public services and housing conditions; free education for all; protection of democratic liberties; equality for women; and a non-aligned foreign policy. The Sandinista Popular Army, based on its own revolutionary forces, replaced Somoza's National Guard. Neighborhood-based Committees to Defend the Revolution, pretty much copied from Cuba, helped with food distribution, medical canvassing, and coordinated neighborhood-based militias.

The Sandinistas founded a National Development Bank to support agriculture and industry, and attracted support from Sweden, France, Spain, Italy, and the USSR. All the help was desperately needed: the Sandinistas faced an embargo as well as a counter-revolutionary war sponsored by Washington.

I went to Nicaragua in 1987 to help the Sandinista Revolution, as part of TecNica – a group of north Americans who offered technical skills to bolster the young revolution. As a worker-expert in computer-based publishing (aka "desktop publishing"), I helped upgrade the Sandinista national newspaper, *Barricada,* using personal computers, laser printers, and plain paper – all readily available on the world market – side-stepping the U.S. effort to strangle the revolution. It was a wonderful opportunity for me, and a fabulous experience: for three years I lived and worked with Sandinistas and ordinary Nicaraguans while witnessing the revolutionary process. Despite grinding poverty amidst the *contra* war, the Nicas harnessed their tenacity and *alegria* (in-grained love of life). For me it was a chance to see and be part of a genuine revolution, even including participation in a neighborhood militia.

The closest I came to "armed struggle" was jamming an antique M1 rifle during an evening militia practice. While on guard we heard noise that turned out to be a mix of family feud and drunken brawl. My other "war-like" experience was the loud *BANG* of mangoes falling on our zinc roof: the first time I heard it I thought the war had finally landed in Managua. I also traveled up to the mountains where the Sandinista guerrillas had built their revolutionary bases, but by the time I got there in 1987, the purpose was to celebrate earlier victories. That was beautiful enough, and my hosts made it "sort of real," by stowing me in the back of a troop truck, where I fell asleep, giving them the chance to scare me awake with a fake emergency. (I wasn't exactly Che Guevara.)

Ordinary daily life in Nicaragua was an education in itself: as part of the volunteer staff at the newspaper, I received the same weekly ration of rice and beans as everyone else. It was a great opportunity to slim down while developing a taste for local herbs and spices. Another internationalist friend and I pooled resources to buy a Honda 50 motorbike, which I used to get to the local market and shop with the local people. Unfortunately my friend Jon

Fyles lost his life on the motorbike in a highway accident a few months after we bought it. This tragedy moved the *Barricada* editors and staff to reach out to Jon's mother with condolences and emotional support. Jon was from Canada. His friends there founded a Jon Fyles Brigade to carry on solidarity with Nicaragua in his name. That was a reminder of Ben Linder, the young University of Washington engineer who was killed by contras while constructing a hydroelectric "micro dam" in the mountains of Jinotega, close to where Sandinista guerrillas had first fought. After Ben's murder President Daniel Ortega shouldered his coffin in a procession after speaking at his funeral. The guest house I stayed in when I first went to Managua with TecNica was named the Ben Linder House.

I saw several other fatal motorbike accidents during my stay in Nicaragua, but I still loved riding, and was luckier than Jon. But one night I finally learned my lesson, when I borrowed another friend's bigger bike – a Honda 750 – for an evening joy ride after a few *tragos* of excellent Nicaraguan *Flor de Caña* rum. I let the front wheel graze a street divider and dumped the bike. An ambulance brought me to a local hospital where Cuban doctors moved *"el internacionalista"* to the front of the line. They found I had a dislocated collar bone which they put in a brace, and sent me home with the admonition to *"hacer el amor boca arriba"* (make love face-up) for at least two weeks. I tried heroically to comply...

Nicaragua was easy to love. The national police called themselves the "sentinels of the people's happiness" *(sentinelas de la alegria del pueblo)*. When I was pulled over for traffic infractions, they were always polite as they confiscated my license, letting me know I could pick it up several days later. *(Gracias, compañero!)* All the main leaders were generally known by their first names. There was a mystique about the 1979 insurrection that toppled the Somoza dictatorship. Somoza – whom President Roosevelt (FDR) referred to as "a son of a bitch, but *our* son of a bitch" – was easy to hate.

The Sandinista anthem was inspiring. My favorite line was *"Luchamos contra el Yanqui, enemigo de la humanidad!"* (We fight against the Yankee, enemy of humanity!) My hosts often cast a worried glance my way as I sang with customary gusto. This line is highly appropriate. Augusto Cesar Sandino was called a "bandit" by the U.S. in 1927, when he led a rebellion against the constant U.S. military occupation during the so-called "Banana Wars" that began in 1898. "Democracy" in Central America, for the U.S., was nothing more than freedom for the United Fruit Company to exploit the local workers and take tons of bananas out at whatever price they wanted. To the

U.S., a "bandit" was anyone who would fight against that arrangement. Sandino was assassinated in 1934 by the National Guard forces of Anastasio Somoza, who then ruled with strong U.S. backing until the Sandinista insurrection of 1979.

The Sandinista revolution was one of several in the region. These revolutions made me believe Vietnam's victory was spreading. I should have realized Ronald Reagan would not just stand by allowing "America's backyard" to be liberated. In 1982 Reagan sent the Marines and Air Force to crush Grenada's New Joint Endeavor for Welfare, Education, and Liberation, or New JEWEL Movement. Reagan then boasted that "America's Back!" after this successful intervention. (Grenada is an island nation with a population of about 100,000, off the coast of Venezuela.) Protests were muted.

In Central America, Reagan used proxies to fight his counterrevolution. Military fascists, who trained at the "School of the Americas" in Georgia, used death squads in El Salvador and Guatemala to slaughter tens of thousands of peasants, as well as a number of north American Catholic nuns and the archbishop of San Salvador. In Nicaragua, the U.S.-supported *contras* – dubbed "freedom fighters" by Reagan – spread terror in the countryside, trying to reverse the Sandinista gains.

In 1979, the same year the Sandinistas triumphed, a revolution broke out in Iran, ending the 26-year dictatorship of Shah Reza Pahlavi. The Shah had been enthroned in 1953 during a CIA-engineered coup against Prime Minister Mossadegh, who had committed the unforgiveable sin of moving to nationalize the Anglo-Iranian Oil Company. Shortly after the 1979 revolution triumphed, young Iranians stormed the U.S. embassy and took 52 hostages. They held the embassy for more than a year and brought defeat and disgrace to President Jimmy Carter. Successor Ronald Reagan hit back hard by fomenting a war between Iran and neighboring Iraq. This conflict dragged on for eight years, resulting in nearly a million deaths and casualties on both sides. The U.S. backed Iraq against Iran, but allowed the war to end in stalemate in 1988. Henry Kissinger famously observed "It's a pity both sides can't lose." At the time, Kissinger also quipped: "The illegal we do immediately. The unconstitutional takes a little longer."

Ever since then, the U.S. has waged either covert or open war against both Iraq and Iran. George H.W. Bush launched the "Desert Storm" invasion against Iraq almost immediately after his inauguration in 1991. Officially the war aimed at toppling Saddam Hussein, but in reality it facilitated U.S. takeover of Iraqi oil. This sudden "shock and awe" invasion morphed into 12 years of brutal sanctions – really a war of attrition. George W. Bush's misdirected retaliation for 9/11, launched in late 2003, was a disastrous and criminal failure, and has dragged on and on. Regardless of claims of "weapons of mass destruction," etc., it was mainly about profits for U.S. oil companies and military contractors, but has caused endless tragedies for ordinary Americans and Iraqis. About Face/Veterans Against the War has mobilized often against the war makers, exposing the lies and telling the truth.[9]

Returning to the topic of Nicaragua in the 1980s, Reagan's people cleverly managed money designated for counter-revolution in Iran to fund the Nicaraguan *contras,* in an illegal operation that became known as "Iran-Contragate." (The "gate" part harkened back to the Watergate scandal that ended Nixon's presidency in 1974.) This time, despite loud protests against obvious violations of U.S. and international law, Reagan survived as "the Teflon president." He managed to keep the *contras* going long enough to strangle Nicaragua's economy and to set the stage for the Sandinistas' electoral defeat in 1990. Reduced backing from the USSR also constituted a major factor. The 1991 collapse of the Soviet Union, caused by unrelenting pressure to maintain the "balance of terror" with the USA, left revolutionary countries like Nicaragua and Cuba without the bastion of support they needed. It also showed the importance of the USSR to the world revolutionary movement, and the enormous cost of its loss. (Close friends and comrades were deeply demoralized by this loss. In at least one case, a comrade resigned from revolutionary activity in tears.)

Decades later, Sandinista President Daniel Ortega has had to fight back against an aggressive campaign to discredit his government as illegitimate and "dictatorial." Nicaragua has had the highest growth rate in Central America in recent years.[10] Annual minimum wage increases at 5–7 percent above inflation, improving workers' living conditions and lifting people out of poverty. The poverty rate fell by 30 percent between 2005 and 2014. The Task Force on Central America reports that for more than a decade Nicaragua has been the safest country in Latin America. Its police force is

---

[9] See Appendix 4: Refusing to Commit War Crimes and Testifying, and Appendix 5: Call for Unconditional Amnesty for Military Resisters to Current U.S. Wars in Iraq, Afghanistan and Pakistan.

[10] Task Force on Central America, http://taskforceamericas.org/statement-in-support-of-nicaragua/

internationally recognized for innovative community policing policies. Unlike neighboring El Salvador, Honduras, and Guatemala, where terrorized families have been fleeing to the U.S. border, Nicaragua has minimal gang violence or organized drug cartels.

The contrast with Honduras is especially interesting. In 2010 the U.S. engineered and sponsored a *coup d'etat* against the popular Honduran President, Mel Zelaya, after he aligned his government with Venezuela and Nicaragua. Since then, tens of thousands of Hondurans have fled in panic from death squads and gangs.

Nicaragua has free health care for all; free education from pre-school through college and graduate school; one month's paid vacation, 13 paid holidays and an extra month's pay each year.

In 2021, during the runup to Nicaragua's November elections, corporate media screamed after the Sandinista government arrested several opposition figures for alleged money laundering. The money in question comes from the National Endowment for Democracy (NED) and the U.S. Agency for International Development (USAID): more than $160 million, according to the USAID website. This "aid" has gone to opposition parties and media, and non-governmental organizations (NGOs). It helped finance a failed coup attempt in 2018, and is meant to strengthen the opposition in the 2021 elections – an *exact* copy of the strategy used in 1990 to engineer the Sandinista electoral defeat. This time the Nicaraguan government established strict accounting laws to force the sums into the open. (For comparison, since the U.S. economy is *1750 times* bigger than Nicaragua's, a similar effort in the U.S. would involve $280 *billion*.)

My friend Gerry Condon of Veterans For Peace, wrote in July 2021 for *LA Progressive,* "Why Do the Media Hate Daniel Ortega?" He said "recent polls show the Ortega government retaining widespread support and easily defeating even a united opposition ticket. They have nothing to fear at the ballot box." After explaining the money laundering issue, he tells of the 2018 attempted coup in Nicaragua – "widespread, coordinated violence, apparently taking the Ortega government by surprise. Barricades blocked many roads, bringing commerce to a halt. A sophisticated social media campaign brought people into the streets with lies about the police killing students. Government buildings were torched. Over 200 people died in street violence over several weeks. Half or more of the dead were Sandinistas, including 24 police. Videos were posted online of Sandinistas being tortured and even burned alive at the barricades."

"Daniel Ortega deflated the attempted coup by showing great restraint," Gerry writes. Ortega "pulled the police back to their barracks. He kept the Army out of the fray. He negotiated with opposition leaders. And he granted amnesty to those who had joined in these violent events. Ortega is now praised for having the wisdom not to overreact – not to cause further violence and chaos. Nonetheless, western media prefers to paint Ortega as an 'authoritarian dictator' who violently represses dissent and jails his political adversaries."

It was a classic CIA "color revolution" that failed. But USAID and NED haven't stopped, and the U.S. Congress has imposed brutal sanctions that punish the Nicaraguan people for supporting their Sandinista government.

Gerry's version of events is backed up by John Perry, of the Council on Hemispheric Affairs, who wrote from Masaya, where he lived during the attempted coup, that "my day-to-day conversations tell me support for government policies remains strong, that hardly anyone wants a return to the roadblocks and violence deployed by government opponents in 2018, and that economic recovery after the damage done then and by the pandemic and hurricanes in 2020 are much bigger priorities than any concerns about recent government action against its opponents."

Other reports debunked the corporate media's version: two major articles by Peter Bolton in *Counter Punch,* and another by Ben Norton in *The Gray Zone.*

Carlos Fonseca Terán, the son of the original founder of the Sandinista National Liberation Front, wrote passionately on July 19, 2021, the 42nd anniversary of Nicaragua's revolution:

"Nicaragua is in the news again. But not for being one of the countries with the greatest reduction in poverty and social inequality… Nor for being the country with the highest level of direct ownership of the means of production by the working class in the Western Hemisphere (more than 50% of GDP and nearly 80% of economic units); nor for being one of the countries in the world that has most reduced illiteracy… and with the largest reduction in infant mortality.

"Nicaragua is not news for being the country in the world that has most reduced the gender gap (from 90th to 12th), the country with the highest presence of women in its cabinet (58.82%), as well as having the fourth highest presence of women in the legislative branch (48.4%) and being the country that most radically applies the criterion of gender equity across its social policies…

"Nor is this country in the news for being among the countries that have most increased electricity coverage (from 53% to 99%) and the one that has most increased its renewable energy sources (from 2% to 90%); nor for being the safest country in Central America and one of the safest in Latin America... Nor is Nicaragua news for having one of the governments in the world with the highest sustained popular support for the longest period of time (with rates around 60% in the last eleven years)...

"In other words," for Fonseca Terán, "the Sandinista government is popular rebellion in power, fighting from the government against the age-old system imposed by the oppressor classes." The U.S. government and corporate media don't like that. I do.

The Sandinista revolution attracted both hardline revolutionary solidarity and supporters who appreciated the features of a relatively soft approach to transformation, like mixed economy and willingness to accept externally imposed rules of the game for elections. This last part backfired for the Sandinistas. Supremely confident of popular support and enthusiasm for the revolution, they basically told their U.S. haters they could win popular elections regardless of interference from Washington. When they lost the 1990 elections, it was an important and tragic lesson. In a sense, the U.S.-backed *contra* war succeeded. A decade of bloody fighting, together with an economic blockade and massive funding for the opposition, was enough to bring an electoral defeat. It was a lesson not to be repeated.

When Mao and the Communist Party took power in China back in 1949, they established People's Democracy, under which "the right of reactionaries to voice their opinions must be abolished and only the people are allowed to have the right to voice their opinions." Mao said "the people" includes the working class, the peasants, the petty bourgeoisie, and national bourgeoisie – not very different from a definition that works for Sandinista Nicaragua. "These classes united to form their own state and elect their own government to carry out a dictatorship over the lackeys of imperialism – the landlord class, the bureaucratic capitalist class – to suppress them, allowing them only to behave properly and not to talk and act wildly. The democratic system is to be carried out within the ranks of the people, giving them freedom of speech, assembly, and association."

People's democracy is endlessly attacked as "authoritarian" by U.S. politicians and media, but I have witnessed it in Nicaragua, and it compares very favorably with the U.S. electoral system, where money rules. In both cases, it is only the relentless and fearless efforts of people fighting for real democracy that holds hope for the future.

Reflections:

Ronald Reagan helped me understand the difference between his "democracy" and ours, when he called the Nicaraguan *contras* "the moral equivalent of our founding fathers." (Washington, Jefferson, *et al,* might be insulted by this comparison.) For me it clarified that Reagan and his cohorts were not fighting *for* true democracy in Nicaragua, but *against* it. I came to realize this as a general principle – just as true in 2021 when the U.S. Agency for International Development and National Endowment for Democracy sabotage societies in the name of democracy and human rights in their favorite enemy countries.

11 – "Democracy" as a Weapon

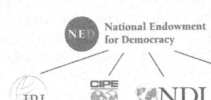

NEWS

Laying the groundwork for change: A closer look at the U.S. role in Nicaragua's social unrest

By Benjamin Waddell / May 1, 2018

...Nicaragua is on the brink of a civic insurrection. For two ...have occupied the

The Secret CIA History of the Iran Coup, 1953

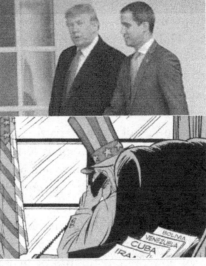

How Washington Hacked Mongolia's Democracy

A Coup in Bolivia, Yet Again

BY
THOMAS FIELD

Bolivia is currently ruled by an unelected president, Jeanine Áñez, whose government is now responsible for nearly two dozen deaths and hundreds of injuries after Evo Morales's overthrow. The situation is dire — but this is far from the first time the country has seen a coup in defense of Bolivia's elites.

U.S. media and politicians use "democracy" as cover for non-stop efforts to discredit, disrupt and overthrow popular revolutions everywhere. In 2018 and 2019, the 45th U.S. president (who lost the popular vote in 2016) "selected" a puppet president to replace Venezuela's democratically elected socialist leader. Everything about the many attempts to topple Venezuela's socialist leaders – first Chavez in 2002 and more recently Maduro – points to a main interest in Venezuela's vast oil reserves, the largest in the world.

For the same reason, the U.S. toppled the democratically elected President Mosaddegh of Iran in 1953, ushering in 26 years of dictatorship under the Shah. In 1954, when the Dulles brothers (Secretary of State John Foster and CIA Director Allen) ousted democratically elected President Arbenz of Guatemala, these Wall Street lawyers were acting on behalf of their major client. The interests of United Fruit were being threatened by land reform, improved wages and working conditions ordered by Arbenz. In that same year Dulles declared the U.S. would not "stand by and let the Vietnamese people vote for communism," especially after three years of "police action" had "saved" half of Korea.

I came to understand the socialist concept that *bourgeois democracy,* is the "dictatorship of the bourgeoisie," *i.e.,* of the business class. No matter how nice the trappings of popular participation might appear, the capitalist political system – in all its various forms and manifestations in different countries – is designed to maintain and protect a system that guarantees the dominance of a minority of big property holders over the rest of the population. The capitalist class controls all the levers of economic activity, and also dominates a state apparatus whose fundamental purpose is to perpetuate capitalist rule. So if a popular revolution happens, it is essential that the new power reverse this process in order to prevent counterrevolution. In the case of Cuba, that's the reason there was an exodus of thousands of landlords and mafiosos after 1959.

China's relatively new policy of "reform and opening up" proposes that under some circumstances a socialist state can make room for capitalists in the otherwise centralized development process. But in this process the role of the centralized state apparatus remains essential. These days China's system and leadership are under constant criticism and attack for not transitioning to a western style electoral system. There's a non-stop western campaign for "democracy and human rights" on behalf of anti-socialist elements trying for a comeback or takeover. My own personal conversations with Chinese friends – here and in China – have convinced me that the majority of people are much better off in China than in the U.S., and the government is responsive to their interests. An example is the Chinese success in lifting 800 million people out of extreme poverty in recent years.

The western media campaigns against "authoritarianism" never acknowledge the constant violations of human rights in the U.S., brutal suppression of voting rights for large portions of the population, or the repeated blatant efforts to stage coups against democratically elected leaders abroad. There is seldom any acknowledgement that the current "democratic" system in the United States was built on a foundation of slavery and genocide. It's really a white power system from top to bottom. Jim Crow laws may be part of the past, but their vestiges remain, not only in the system of mass incarceration, but in constant efforts to suppress voting rights for people of color. The result is that systemic racism is enshrined in Washington, DC, and in state capitals and city halls across the USA.

While the official media criticize "violations of democratic rights" in China, Venezuela, Nicaragua, Bolivia, etc., etc. – essentially *any* country that does not conform to the "Washington consensus" – the U.S. system has elaborate guarantees to ensure that big money rules. In the midst of the 2020 surge of popular energy to overturn the rule of Trump and the Republican Party, I could never forget that the entire electoral apparatus, plus the courts, are completely rigged to protect and preserve the capitalist system. The constant campaign to limit the right of the poor and people of color to vote is often called "preventing electoral fraud." Meanwhile genuinely fraudulent elections secured the victory of George W. Bush in both 2000 and 2004. And in 2016, the results in Florida, Georgia, and Ohio were subject to question – at least. The infamous Electoral College is the linchpin of a constitutional arrangement that has guaranteed disproportionate electoral representation to states with smaller, more rural populations over those with large cities. This distribution also tends to favor former slave states. So the heritage of slavery lives on in a quasi-democratic system that disenfranchises millions.

My first political act after joining the Spring 1967 anti-war march in San Francisco was to gather petition signatures to get the Peace and Freedom Party on the ballot. The effort was successful, and the PFP has retained ballot status in California ever since. I also went out gathering signatures and knocking on doors for Bernie Sanders and two local socialist candidates in the Bronx – just like thousands of other DSA members. It's a reminder of what Malcolm X said: "If you want to make a revolution, you must go door-to-door!" But it's an up-hill battle against big money and big party machines designed to control the game from start to finish.

The "winner-take-all" system discourages competition with the two official parties, both of which are funded lavishly by the rich and by large corporations. Ever since the 2010 Citizens United decision by the Supreme Court, corporations have "free speech" rights (as "persons"), so they can contribute whatever amount they want to political campaigns with no obligation to report such contributions. Big money monopolizes the electoral system in the U.S., frustrating the endless efforts of progressives by forcing voters to elect "the lesser of two evils."

Over the decades socialists have made valiant efforts to take power through elections, and then introduce socialism using the existing system. It's like fool's gold. First you get it in your hand, then you discover it's not what you thought it was. For example, in England after World War 2, the Labour Party won the elections. Instead of introducing socialism they basically ran the capitalist state for the bankers. They proposed votes in Parliament on some socialist measures, and even got some progressive things done, like establishing the national health care system. But socialism never took root in England. The same was true in other European countries at various times in the 20th century. We need to be aware of these precedents, even as we strive to elect socialist candidates.

Chile under Socialist President Salvador Allende (1971-73) provides another example. Allende's Popular Unity government implemented many socialist measures, and had the strong support of the people. But Nixon, Kissinger and the CIA worked hand-in-glove with International Telephone and Telegraph (ITT) and the big U.S. copper companies there, as well as right-wingers in the national assembly, and their partners in the armed forces. They waged a destabilization campaign to cause economic and political chaos, and at a pre-appointed moment the military stepped in with a heavy hand. Allende was dead and all his close associates and political allies were jailed, killed or exiled; a brutal dictatorship took over and ruled for two decades.

These situations expose the vulnerabilities of electoral politics. During the Russian Revolution the Bolsheviks called for workers' councils – the soviets – to seize power. They abolished the old state structure that had served the czars and the capitalists, and built a new state. The workers and peasants who made up the rank-and-file in the armed forces went on strike and then deserted, weapons in hand. They ultimately left the old military an empty shell, except for elite units that survived and mobilized against the new workers' state. This counterrevolutionary mobilization failed because the new revolu-tionary leadership created a people's army to defend the new state. The police were replaced with a new police system dedicated to the new order. The same happened to the court system, which had been used to repress and imprison millions of poor people in Russia and its dependent nationalities. Old Russia had been a "prison house of nations," because the system of repression fell most heavily on people of Russia's many oppressed nationalities – not so different from the U.S. today.

After the revolution the new state took a new name: no longer was it simply Russia, but instead a *Union of Soviet Socialist Republics.* "Soviet" is the Russian word for council, in this case *workers' council.* There were workers' councils and peasants' councils everywhere the revolution took place. These councils *replaced* the old decision-making bodies, which were rotten and corrupt – pretty much like the Congress, state assemblies and city councils in the USA. The "representatives" in these bodies were most often pre-selected by the local or national elite, and then "elected" in a system that prevented the majority from proposing other representatives. The system made it impossible for large numbers of people to vote. They called it democracy, but it was an elaborate system designed to *prevent* real democracy – much like here in the USA today.

This lesson from history is relevant today. As we consider how to end police brutality and make a Green New Deal happen, we need to look beyond elections. As workers and allies, we need our own organizations and our own democracy to take power. We need to start with what we have. In addition to
seats in Congress, city councils and state assemblies, we also have unions, community organizations, popular assemblies, and mass mobilizations.

I had this experience with the South Bronx Community Congress during the Obama years. As a coalition of tenant organizations, unionists and other community groups, we held annual People's Assemblies at Hostos Community College in the south Bronx. On the agenda were struggles against workplace racism. Marches took place against poverty and violence, and for jobs. We also launched a campaign to save 17 Bronx post offices from threatened closing.

In 2011 these campaigns merged with a citywide movement against anti-people budget cuts in New York. In March of that year thousands marched from City Hall to Wall Street and back. A week later a thousand workers occupied the state capitol in Albany. In May there was a more massive march, organized by the teachers union and its allies. In mid-June the NYC public workers union mobilized thousands of public sector workers; the next day the NYC Building Trades Council staged a giant protest of construction workers. This was the first large labor march in decades to break through police barricades intended to hem them in and blunt their message.

Then came "Bloombergville," an encampment near New York's City Hall – a massive "sit-in" lasting several weeks, to protest Mayor Bloomberg's austerity budget. Inspired by gigantic occupations of public squares in Egypt, Tunisia, Spain, Greece and Wisconsin, these mobilizations in turn stimulated Occupy Wall Street – an outpouring of "the 99%" that lasted for weeks and spread across the country. Apparently leaderless, the mobilization inspired "copy-cat" occupations in cities across the country and beyond borders. On the west coast the longshore workers union joined hands with the Occupy movement to shut down ports from San Diego to Vancouver, BC.

This kind of popular explosion burst across the country again in the spring of 2020, stronger than ever, in the wake of police murders of Black people. The question arises: How will this type of popular power replace the existing official structures? It can happen when the old system of governing no longer works, and this becomes obvious to large numbers of people, and the economy has also failed. We must be ready with the organizations of popular power and revolutionary leadership.

The exact way a revolutionary transition may happen is unpredictable. It depends on the specific way the old system deteriorates and falls apart. That this will happen *is* predictable. Millions were disillusioned by the lavish bailouts of banks following the crash and meltdown of 2008. And it's clear that U.S. control has diminished in other parts of the world. The many U.S.

efforts to stamp out rebellions and reverse revolutions have caused it to become over-extended. More and more soldiers and sailors in the U.S. military have become disillusioned and refuse to continue acting as hired guns of imperialism. Over time the U.S. rulers lack the power to hold the empire together, and the need for a new system will become ever more evident.

Meanwhile the U.S. working class is changing. The old post-WW2 working class, with privileged pay conditions for some, is disappearing.

Workers in the USA are being pushed down to the conditions of the rest of the world. And the composition of the working class has changed, with equal numbers of women and men, and nearly as many people of color as whites. These conditions will help overcome racism and sexism in our own ranks – major tools used to keep workers divided and weak in the past. These changes will help revive the fighting spirit of the U.S. working class, and conditions for change will rapidly mature. It has begun to happen in the wake of the coronavirus pandemic and the resulting economic meltdown.

But revolutionary leadership is needed. We need to combine forces and tactics, to sustain and multiply the popular forces in motion, and move beyond the "politics of the possible." This emphatically does *not* mean we should never run candidates for office, or build a mass socialist party. We definitely should, and thus win as many people as possible to understand and support socialism. But we must be clear that to actually achieve the goal of socialism, it will take more.

We need to know *in advance* that when socialists win elections, the real struggle will just begin. A mass movement, ready to defend our gains and *change the power structure* will be needed. Dismantling the military, for example, can only happen if the soldiers organize themselves to resist. And reorganizing production and distribution on a mass scale will require a multi-layered struggle.

This way of thinking has helped the Chavistas and Bolivarians in Venezuela to persist. In 2017, faced with constant U.S.-backed counterrevolutionary efforts and threats of military invasion, the Bolivarian government replaced the old national assembly with a Constituent Assembly that is in turn based on people's councils which have sprung up across the country. While U.S. economic sanctions and a well-organized campaign of capital flight has caused skyrocketing inflation, so the Venezuelan currency is essentially worthless, the government has responded with a series of measures. It provides guaranteed food deliveries to the population through the people's councils, and has instituted an electronic currency to maintain at least part of its oil business, with help from Russia and China. The Bolivarian government has moved to integrate representation of the people's councils with the military – making it a *people's army*, ready for rapid mass popular mobilization for national defense when necessary. This has frustrated several U.S.-backed attempted coups.

There is also hope that Nicaragua may one day realize the dream of building a new canal through Nicaragua, with China's help. This could make large-scale oil sales from Venezuela to China viable, and also give a big boost to my Nicaragüita. Nothing would please me more than to see China breaking the blockade, sanctions and embargoes against Venezuela, Nicaragua, and Cuba! Of course the USA can be counted on to do everything in its power to stop such a defeat to its global dominance. But U.S. power is more limited than ever before. It is not the all-powerful global hegemon it once was, and would like to continue to be.

Reflections:

My life on the left has been, and continues to be, a marvelous adventure. Being a revolutionary is like being a midwife for the future. While there is blood and pain, its essence is hope and excitement for a future we can begin to see ahead of us. And while there is endless cause for anger and frustration, my vision for the future is positive. We are creating a better world, and I have seen glimpses of it that are truly inspiring.

12 – Socialism and the Green New Deal

Alexandria Ocasio-Cortez sparked an unstoppable movement for a Green New Deal, meeting with the Sunrise Movement in Nancy Pelosi's congressional office, Nov. 13, 2018.

"It is impossible to exaggerate the awesome nature of the challenge we face: to determine, within the next few years, whether organized human society can survive in anything like its present form. Global warming is already a prime factor in destroying species at a rate not seen for 65 million years. There is no time to delay changing course radically to avert major catastrophe."
—*Noam Chomsky*

It has been well known for at least four decades that climate change poses a significant threat to the earth. Major polluters like the owners and executives of Big Oil knew it so well they have spent billions on climate denial and fake science, to delay the day of reckoning. They have also funded several generations of corrupt politicians to assure free rein for polluters. A friend in the White House appointed oil lobbyists to manage natural resources and cancelled environmental protections.

Now we're in a full-scale crisis. The latest scientific reports indicate we have less than *12 years* to fix the problem, or otherwise face major disaster and possible extinction as a species. Disasters keep happening – the fires in California that have wiped out communities, the volcanoes and floods in farm country that have destroyed both crops and communities, the hurricanes that have wreaked devastation in Texas, Florida, and Puerto Rico, and on and on. Hurricane-related deaths in Puerto Rico exceeded those caused in New York on September 11, 2001 – for which the reaction was "endless war."

Meanwhile the U.S. war machine has become the biggest polluter on the planet, and the largest consumer of fossil fuels. Its main job is to assure U.S. control of the infinitely profitable oil industry. If the cost of military protection for oil extraction and transport were included in the cost per tank of gasoline, millions of people would stop driving because of the high cost. Instead this massive tax subsidy diverts the majority of public funds away from health, education, social welfare, industrial policy, and all the rest, to more endless war.[11] Incidentally, the military budget does *not* include the casualties; countless military veterans have seen their lives destroyed needlessly and criminally.

So the current economic and social system – capitalism – cannot be expected to fix the problem of climate change. It has been dedicated for decades to *preventing* meaningful solutions, such as electric cars, public transportation, and development of a renewable energy system adequate to avoid pollution. There is simply too much profit and power spun off by the existing profit-based system. It will need to be replaced, or at minimum significantly transformed, to get a solution.

Socialism is back in fashion these days. Polls indicate a majority of people under thirty prefer it to capitalism. Lots of gray heads like it too. We are increasingly aware that the profit system is failing us, and threatening our future. Many retirees depend on monthly Social Security checks, and now a huge percentage want universal health care: "Medicare for All." These common sense ideas are often denounced as "creeping socialism." This helps explain why people like socialism more and more. Perhaps equally important, there is a growing realization that socialism is vastly more democratic than capitalism, despite all the propaganda to the contrary. It would be interesting to see how many of the current crop of corrupt politicians could win re-election without money from big oil, big pharma, big banks, and insurance companies.

A movement is emerging for a "Green New Deal," sparked by Alexandria Ocasio-Cortez (AOC), a dynamic and fiery young former bar tender and self-proclaimed socialist who is shaking up Congress and inspiring young and old

---

[11] See "U.S. Fossil Fuel Subsidies Exceed Pentagon Spending," by Tim Dickinson, *Rolling Stone,* May 8, 2019.

across the country. She proposes changing election funding, taxing the rich at a rate of 70 percent, slashing the Pentagon budget, and using those trillions to convert the economy away from fossil fuels.

Right-wingers have been screaming like stuck pigs, led by their president, who swore "there will never be socialism in this country." A battle is brewing. Young people are mobilizing. An organizing letter for a March 15, 2019 international youth strike said:

"We are going to change the fate of humanity, whether you like it or not. United we will rise until we see climate justice... The youth of this world have started to move and we will not rest again." The youth take seriously scientific predictions that there is less than 12 years to save the planet from floods, fires and even worse natural disasters caused by climate change.

The Green New Deal proposal is transformative. *(See Appendix 8.)* It does not directly call for socialism – just for whatever it takes to stop using fossil fuels. This might only involve a conversion of the energy industry to renewables, an expansion and intensification of public transport, transition to electric vehicles from gas guzzlers, construction or conversion of millions of affordable homes with solar panels, and a drastic reduction of the biggest consumer of fossil fuels – the U.S. Department of "Defense." We would, of course, need to shut down oil pipelines, and end "mountain removal" coal operations. Food production would have to change to sustainable methods, shifting away from chemical fertilizers; much less beef, and massive mulching to re-capture carbon nutrients for the soil and get them out of the atmosphere.

Financing the Green New Deal may require a transformation of the banking and credit systems. New public banks might need to be established, or old banks nationalized. Definitely creeping socialism! Some moderates, including Thomas Friedman and the New York Times editorial board, think a version of GND can happen without sacrificing the profit system.[12] Maybe so, but they'd better hurry.

Republicans are rabidly upset, foaming at the mouth. "They want to take your pickup truck! They want to rebuild your home! They want to take away your hamburgers! This is what Stalin dreamt about but never achieved!" They call it a watermelon: "Green on the outside, deep, deep red communist on the inside."[13]

---

[12] *NY Times,* editorial Feb. 23, 2019. Thomas Friedman, Jan. 8, 2019.

[13] *New Yorker,* Mar. 3, 2019

Truthfully, that doesn't sound so bad to me, and inspired me to join the Democratic Socialists of America. The DSA membership process asked if AOC was your main reason for joining. I had to admit it. But it's not just her strong and courageous leadership. DSA grew from slightly less than 6,000 members in 2016 to more than 80,000 after two primary presidential runs by Bernie Sanders, and continues to grow fast. Of 100 people at my first local membership meeting, about 20 were new. At that rate DSA may double or triple soon, making it the largest socialist organization ever in the USA. It will need to be even bigger, and ever bolder, but that could happen. *(See Appendix 9: "An Ecosocialist Green New Deal.")*

Even getting close to a GND will involve a huge fight – a wide range of struggles at local, regional and national levels. While politicians delay and dither, people are taking action. Tactics include mass blockades of oil pipelines, occupations of politicians' offices, and canvassing door-to-door for initiatives to convert energy companies to public utilities – like California's Pacific Gas & Electric, which filed for bankruptcy following the devastating Camp fires of 2018. Preparing for and recovering from natural disasters has become a mass movement. In the wake of the coronavirus pandemic, this mass movement is a *rescue effort* for society as a whole.

Opponents of GND say it would "ruin the economy" as we know it – no more massive profits for big oil, big auto or big banking. (What a shame!) Most western societies have survived and thrived on reckless, destructive growth for generations. Many traditional jobs would disappear along with the fossil fuel industry, and need to be replaced. The real motivation for recent wars – control of the world's oil supply – would wither away. All of this would require a coordinated economic conversion on a grand scale. The new way of doing things might look and feel a lot like socialism.

But it will take a *real* fight – a *revolutionary* struggle. It could lead to much better jobs for many more people: jobs building the new infrastructure, retrofitting homes, schools and businesses; rebuilding the energy grid and retrofitting metropolitan and regional energy providers to use renewable energy, and more. We might hark back to the hydroelectric dams that were built during the New Deal of the 1930s, with something better. New technology could make it possible to harness the energy of *ocean tides,* in addition to the sun and the wind.

There is a big difference between the Green New Deal and the first one, back in the 1930s. That one left out people who were not white. This one, according to AOC, promises "to promote justice and equity by stopping current, preventing future, and repairing historic oppression of indigenous peoples, communities of color, migrant communities, deindustrialized communities, depopulated rural communities, the poor, low-income workers, women, the elderly, the unhoused, people with disabilities, and youth." The GND resolution specifies "directing investments to spur economic development, deepen and diversify industry and business in local and regional economies, and build wealth and community ownership, while prioritizing high-quality job creation and economic, social and environmental benefits in frontline and vulnerable communities, and deindustrialized communities, that may otherwise struggle with the transition away from greenhouse gas intensive industries."

That's a mouthful, but *that's revolutionary!* And it will take a revolution to achieve it. As Naomi Klein wrote, "The shift from one power system to another must be more than a mere flipping of a switch... It must be accompanied by a power correction in which the old injustices that plague our societies are righted once and for all. That's how you build an army of solar warriors."[14]

The "warriors" Klein mentions are the people who will mobilize for jobs and basic public services that work, for decent housing, for land redistribution, which is "nothing less than the unfinished business of the most powerful liberation movements of the past two centuries, from civil rights to feminism to Indigenous sovereignty." Winning these things "could deliver the equitable redistribution of agricultural lands that was supposed to follow independence from colonial rule and dictatorship; it could bring the jobs and homes that Martin Luther King, Jr., dreamed of; it could bring jobs and clean water to Native communities; it could at last turn on the lights and running water in every South African township. Such is the promise of a Marshall Plan for the Earth."

Winning all this is the work of revolution. Getting to socialism can only happen if capitalism breaks down, and if a large percentage of the population cannot go on as before, and if there is leadership willing and able to manage the transition. That is, it needs a crisis, a mass movement, and visionary leaders who are strong enough to overcome large scale resistance from the right.

Bernie Sanders found a powerful partner in AOC, and others are emerging. It was the Sanders campaign that brought us AOC and the others

---

[14] Naomi Klein, *This Changes Everything: Capitalism vs The Climate*, 2014, p. 399.

like her, and the hope that there will be many more. He was the one that excited young people by the millions, making them want and believe in "a political revolution" in this country. It's a great idea – even if it's just a start – and potentially the start of something very big.

Bernie Sanders has done a lot to popularize socialism, but he didn't really define it.

The key thing about socialism is cooperative and democratic control of the economy for the benefit of society. A *political* revolution might consist of getting a democratic socialist majority in Congress, electing a socialist president, some socialist governors, mayors, city councils, state assemblies and so on. That would definitely get things going. But we should be realistic. Such a revolution would also have to transform the old state apparatus – the military, cops and courts. We would need to take over the "commanding heights" of the economy. What are the "commanding heights"? Banks top the list, because they control most major corporations. Then there is the military-industrial complex. President Eisenhower warned about it in the 1950s. Now it dominates, with big oil and the banks, all aspects of economic planning and policy making.

A basic socialist measure would be to expropriate the banks, insurance, energy and rail transport industries, as well as the military-industrial complex and big pharma. The result would be control of a large majority of all economic activity, either centrally or at state or local levels. A start, but there's more.

Another key factor is self-determination for oppressed nations, especially African-American people whose ancestors built a huge part of the wealth of this country after they were dragged here in chains; also the Native peoples from whom *all* the land and its wealth were taken; and Mexican peoples who were dispossessed and driven out of their homes and are now vilified as immigrants or "illegals." Both Puerto Rico and Hawaii would have the right to demand complete independence, or whatever free association they might choose. A socialist government would grant either independence or special status to these nations, respecting their right to reparations and affirmative action, as well as the option to determine whether to be part of the new socialist society or to have their own political entities with support and recognition from the new socialist state.

Getting all this might take a miracle, but let's take another look. The Green New Deal, as Republicans have screamed, can be considered a "socialist plot," but with a special character. It is a serious proposal to save the planet. Nothing less will be enough. As people by the millions become aware of this reality, many things can happen. Strikes and sit-ins by young people will spread and intensify. Workers can mobilize on a large scale, shutting down or taking over work places, ports, and entire cities. They can join with farmers, unemployed people and youth – *everyone* – in massive marches to demand change. Soldiers can shut down military bases across the country and around the world. That would have some impact!

In the late 19th century common people thought socialism was good and capitalism was evil. Common sense again. People who rob and lie and cheat were bad, and people who fought them were good. Take Eugene Debs – a worker who rose to lead the American Railway Union, organized a national strike in 1893 over working conditions and pay that brought the railroads to a halt for more than a month. He then was jailed for "ordering, directing, aiding, assisting, or abetting" it. While in prison Debs had time to study. He learned about socialism there. When asked later "What is Socialism?" he answered: "It recognizes the equality in men [and women]." Debs helped found the Socialist Party, and ran for president in 1912, getting nearly a million votes. In 1916 he was again in jail, this time for speaking out against World War I. "I am opposed to every war but one," he said. "I am for that war with heart and soul, and that is the worldwide war of the social revolution. In that war I am prepared to fight in any way the ruling class may make necessary, even to the barricades."

In 1920 Debs again ran for president, while in prison, charged with sedition. In a speech in 1918 he declared "We are going to destroy all enslaving and degrading capitalist institutions and re-create them as free and humanizing institutions." Newspapers called him a dictator and a traitor. Explaining his opposition and refusal to fight in World War I, he said: "The master class has always declared the wars; the subject class has always fought the battles. The master class has had all to gain and nothing to lose, while the subject class has had nothing to gain and all to lose – especially their lives." For this he was convicted and jailed.

World War I was a turning point. After emerging as a world power following the Spanish-American War of 1898, the U.S. leadership waited while the European powers tore each other apart for three years in trench warfare. Then it stepped in to help Britain and France win against Germany. Meanwhile Russia had a revolution, which nearly spread to Germany. The U.S. was suddenly a world power. It joined the older imperialists in opposing the Russian revolution.

Debs said, "I heartily support the Russian Revolution without reservation." He wrote in 1919 that "The reign of capitalism and militarism has made of all peoples inflammable material. They are ripe and ready for the change, the great change which means the rise and triumph of the workers, the end of exploitation, of war and plunder, and the emancipation of the race... Let us all help its coming and pave the way for it by organizing the workers industrially and politically to conquer capitalism and usher in the day of the people."

Debs continued: "In Russia and Germany our valiant comrades are leading the proletarian revolution, which knows no race, no color, no sex, and no boundary lines. They are setting the heroic example for worldwide emulation. Let us, like them, scorn and repudiate the cowardly compromisers within our own ranks, challenge and defy the robber class power, and fight it out on that line to victory or death!"[15]

In the 1930s there were lots of revolutionaries in the USA – mostly communists, but also socialists, radical pacifists – thousands of them intensely involved in organizing and leading industrial unions, unemployed councils, anti-eviction struggles, anti-racist and anti-fascist movements. The left at that time was focused on bottom-up democracy in the unions and working class communities – both Black and white – across the country. They also waged strong and effective campaigns against racism. They were the only allies of Black people during the Jim Crow years, when there was extreme segregation and lynching. The Depression exposed the failure of capitalism, and the surging left was inspired by the dramatic growth and socialist success in the USSR. It was in that cauldron that FDR launched the first New Deal, which was really a series of emergency measures designed to save capitalism from itself, and give ordinary people some relief. That earlier New Deal is a good starting model for AOC's Green New Deal.

I got my first union job in high school, as a stocker in a supermarket. I liked the union but didn't think much about it. Later I noticed we got periodic pay raises and health benefits, plus a grievance procedure if something happened at work. Now I enjoy a regular Social Security check – glad it was fought for and won during the 1930s. My father hated unions. He was a "rugged individualist" like most people in the far west of this country at that time. He thought the unions were commie fronts. I didn't think much

---

[15] *From* The Class Struggle: Devoted to International Socialism, *February 1919, Vol.III No.1, edited by Eugene V. Debs, Louis C. Fraina and Ludwig Lore. (https://www.marxists.org/archive/debs/works/1919/daypeople.htm)*

about that at the time, but considering who did much of the organizing work to build the unions, I later realized he was at least partly right.

I picked up on the legacy of the left during the late sixties and early seventies, thanks to "old timers" in Canada. The "godfather" or war resister exiles, Bill Spira, migrated from the U.S. to Canada during the witch hunt of the 1950s – a tidal wave of anti-communist hysteria and repression designed to "save the world from communism." Bill linked me up with other old leftists who were still organizing and leading bottom-up democratic unions in Canada. Their struggles and stories connected me to that legacy.

Back then being socialist or communist was almost cool. *Reds,* the 1981 blockbuster movie starring Warren Beatty, captures some of this. The story was set during the period of World War 1 and the 1917 Russian Revolution and its aftermath. At that time the victory of socialism was recognized as the historic arrival of true democracy for the workers and oppressed people – the millions who lived a semi-slave existence in the colonies of Africa and Asia, Latin America, and the plantations and prisons of the U.S. South. Other movies and novels also captured the anti-capitalist spirit of the times – like *The Grapes of Wrath,* a heart-wrenching story of poor dirt farmers driven off the land in the "Dust Bowl" of Oklahoma, heading west to California; *Modern Times* and *The Great Dictator* by Charlie Chaplin. *Casablanca,* the classic 1942 anti-fascist movie, can be considered part of this genre.

Casablanca shows another aspect of the period: the anti-fascist underground movement throughout Europe that resisted the German Nazis and the fascists in France, Spain and Italy. All of these were allied with the Soviet Union, even though the Soviet government was not able to offer much support, other than waging a victorious war effort against the Nazis' blitzkrieg that was meant to end socialism once and for all.

Another valuable and fascinating movie about that time is *1900,* by Bernardo Bertolucci, which tells about the fight of Italy's workers and peasants against fascism. These stories convey the popular character of the anti-fascist movements that swept Europe at the time, making socialism a real possibility if fascism could be defeated.

These movies brought those times alive for me. The rightwing forgers of "the American Century" had to crush and falsify this legacy – a genuine threat to their version of the "American Dream," which depended on suppressing communism at home and abroad, painting it as tyranny.

The realization of all this caught up with me during the Vietnam war. It only dawned on me in the mid-sixties, but looking back at that time I could remember as a child hearing the name of John Foster Dulles on the radio. He was loudly denouncing the communists for "taking over" Asia. That was 1954. Dulles declared that America would not stand by and let the Vietnamese people vote for communism, especially after three years of "police action" had "saved" half of Korea. John Foster Dulles and his brother Allen had been Wall Street lawyers who represented the United Fruit Company. In 1953 they engineered the overthrow of Guatemala's first democratic government after it moved to raise wages for banana workers there. John Foster Dulles was Eisenhower's Secretary of State, while his brother Allen headed the CIA.

These parallels made a lot of things fit together for me later. The artificial division between North and South Vietnam was agreed to be temporary at the Geneva Convention in 1954, with elections planned for two years later. All observers knew Ho Chi Minh would win the elections. So in a grand gesture of "defending South Vietnam's self-determination" for a government it created, the U.S. reneged on the agreement, leaving its puppets in power, and opting for continued war. It lasted another 22 years until April 30, 1975, when Vietnam's national liberation forces marched triumphantly into Saigon while the U.S. embassy was evacuated by helicopter. *(See Appendix 1.)*

These things helped me understand that the "free world" the U.S. was so determined to defend wasn't really all that free, and certainly wasn't very democratic. It became a quest for me to find out and understand how all this happened, and what it was covering up. Here's what I found.

Right after WW2, when the U.S., Britain and France had been allied with the USSR and they jointly defeated Nazi Germany, the "red scare" ensued. U.S. leaders rushed to limit the spread of communism and socialism abroad, and stamp out reds at home. A "witch hunt" and massive repression was launched against communists and "fellow travelers." Anyone suspected even of sympathizing with communism or socialism was driven out of unions, Hollywood, government jobs, and more. During the Depression Franklin Roosevelt had instituted quasi-socialist policies – the New Deal, Social Security, the right of workers to join unions – in order to stop worker rebellions that threatened the capitalist system, which was near collapse in the wake of the crash of 1929 and the Great Depression that followed. Socialists and communists played a big role in organizing and leading the industrial unions that formed in the 1930s – steel workers, miners, auto, electrical and textile workers, and many others. And they mobilized strongly in the war against Nazism, supporting the U.S. alliance with the USSR.

While the USA emerged as the main victor of the war, hysteria grew against the other winner. The Soviet Union had fought and won on the ground against the Nazis, suffering 27 million deaths and the obliteration of its industries west of the Volga river.[16] In the process the USSR helped replace Nazi-sponsored governments in eastern Europe. In western Europe the anti-Nazi underground had played an important role, especially in France and Italy. There was a great fear in Washington that these anti-fascist forces would push for socialism. And in China, a revolution led by the Chinese Communist Party was taking over, bringing the common people to power for the first time in the world's most populous country.

These developments led to the red scare and the witch hunt. Howard Zinn provides details in his *People's History of the United States,* and shows how the red scare turned things upside down, making socialists and communists into devils. But while tens of thousands of red lives were destroyed in the U.S. – and millions more around the world – the red scare couldn't last. The Big Lie began to unravel in the 1960s, with the surge of the Civil Rights and anti-war movements. Martin Luther King, Jr., speaking on April 4, 1967, said "the greatest purveyor of violence in the world today [is] my own government." He went on to say: "What do the peasants think as we ally ourselves with the landlords and as we refuse to put any action into our many words concerning land reform?"

King said, "I am as deeply concerned about our own troops there as anything else. For it occurs to me that what we are submitting them to in Vietnam is not simply the brutalizing process that goes on in any war where armies face each other and seek to destroy. We are adding cynicism to the process of death, for they must know after a short period there that none of the things we claim to be fighting for are really involved... and the more sophisticated surely realize that we are on the side of the wealthy, and the secure, while we create a hell for the poor."

King's bold and prophetic words exposed the Big Lie. A year later, to the day, he was shot dead in Memphis.

So what makes socialists and communists – all revolutionaries – so frightening and devilish?

Revolutionaries are on the side of the workers and the poor, and fight capitalist exploitation. The word "communist" has the same root as

---

[16] See *The Untold History of the United States,* by Oliver Stone and Peter Kuznick, Chapter 3, "World War II: Who Really Defeated Germany?"

"community" and "common." The basic goal of revolutionaries is to build a human community where things are shared in common. That's the way it has been for most of human history – take for example the indigenous peoples who inhabited our continents before the European invasion. They didn't know about private property till the invaders took their land! The fact that we organize and fight for community over exploitation is what capitalists hate and fear.

In Vietnam, Ho Chi Minh and the National Liberation Front mobilized the peasants and workers of their country against the most powerful military machine history had ever seen. They won, proving that "the power of the people is greater than the man's technology," like Bobby Seale had said. As a leader of the Black Panther Party, Bobby Seale also said: "They came down on us because we had a grassroots, real people's revolution, complete with the programs, complete with the unity, complete with the working coalitions, where we crossed racial lines."

I visited the Black Panthers' headquarters in Oakland in the mid-1970s after I returned from exile in Canada. I was impressed by two things: the depth and extent of their social programs – free breakfast for children, schools and community health clinics – and the number of their members who were killed by the police. At that time the Panthers were operating the Oakland Community School, one of a network of Liberation Schools, which received an award in 1977 from the California Governor and Legislature for "having set the standard for the highest level of elementary education in the state."

FBI Director J. Edgar Hoover called the Panthers "the greatest threat to the internal security of the country," and moved to destroy them. A major duty for the rest of the U.S. left at that time was to defend the Panthers. It was not easy. Hoover and then-President Nixon mobilized at every level through the infamous *COINTEL* (counterintelligence) program to infiltrate, harass, prosecute and kill them. But as Bobby Seale also famously said, "You can jail a revolutionary, but you cannot jail the revolution."

Still, the *COINTEL* program wiped out a generation of leaders and organizers of the Black liberation movement, and terrorized its base, along with many other progressive people. That was a victory for Nixon, even though he was forced to resign in disgrace in 1974. It made it easier for Ronald Reason to attack the unions, and rewrite the history of the U.S. war in Vietnam after he won the elections in 1980. *Rambo* movies came out one after another in the 1980s, recapturing popular consciousness from such anti-war movies as *Apocalypse Now,* while Reagan boldly declared "America's back!" following his super-macho invasion of tiny Grenada in 1982.

Reagan came to power in 1981 with a program of smashing the unions, attacking the poor, and "fighting communism in our backyard." He also declared a "war on drugs," which translated into cops descending on Black youth, frisking them and arresting them for small quantities of marijuana. They didn't go after white kids much, even though later reports indicated there was more illegal drug use among whites. The result was mass incarceration of young people of color – a convenient alternative to the Jim Crow system that had been pushed back by the civil rights movement of the sixties.

Reagan scared a lot of people on the left. But on May 3, 1981, a new coalition, the People's Anti-War Mobilization launched "an opening shot of a new progressive movement," with more than 100,000 people marching in Washington, and major actions held in other cities, against Reagan's military buildup and adventures in Central America. I had been out of the country in 1969 and 1970; I missed the massive mobilizations against the Vietnam war in those years. So the May 3, 1981 demonstration was the biggest ever for me. Then in September I joined the giant Solidarity Day march of half a million workers protesting Reagan's attack on PATCO – the Professional Air Traffic Controllers Organization – Reagan's opening shot against the unions. But more than Solidarity Day marches would be needed to stop Reagan.

There was an effort to follow these important mass rallies with an All Peoples Congress convention in Detroit in October, where more than 100 labor, social, and political organizations came together to map a strategy against Reagan's attacks at home and abroad. The Congress drew about 2,000 delegates from across the country. The purpose was to forge a new working class movement against capitalism and imperialism. It wasn't enough to stop Reagan, but was a hint and a new beginning.

During this time I was inspired by Black anti-war activists and resisters, both in and out of the U.S. military. One was Clarence Thomas, a rank-and-file leader of the International Longshore Workers Union (ILWU) Local 10, in San Francisco. I first encountered him as a leader of the Black Students Union at San Francisco State College back in the mid-1960s. The BSU woke me up to the reality of the draft and the war at that time. This group and others, in addition to the Black Panthers, can take a big share of the credit for spawning the enormous GI resistance movement in Vietnam, as well as on U.S. military bases both in the USA and across the globe.

Clarence and Local 10 were instrumental in many historic struggles. In 1984 they shut down the port of San Francisco rather than unload cargo from apartheid South Africa. Six years later anti-apartheid leader Nelson Mandela won his freedom and became president of the Republic of South Africa, ending half a millennium of brutal, racist colonialism. Reagan and the apartheid leaders had called Mandela a "terrorist."

In 2011 ILWU joined hands with the Occupy movement to shut down the West Coast. Nearly every May Day (May 1, International Workers Day), the San Francisco dock workers take the day off to march. It recalls the 1934 San Francisco General Strike, when ILWU shut down the ports on the west coast for 83 days. All west coast ports were unionized as a result. This historic action, along with the Teamsters' strike in Minneapolis, and others in Ohio and Michigan, nearly all led by communists or socialists, forged the Congress of Industrial Organizations – the CIO.

This can happen again. And it can spread like wildfire. While unions are weaker in the U.S. now, after several decades of "globalization," which took millions of manufacturing jobs away, the struggle is alive and intensifying. In 2018 tens of thousands of teachers struck *and won*, first in West Virginia, then Oklahoma, Colorado, and Arizona – all so-called "red" states, where Republicans dominate. These teachers fought and won on their own, without official union backing. An official teacher strike also won in Chicago in 2018, and the Los Angeles and Oakland public school teachers walked out and won in early 2019. Service workers at McDonalds and other fast-food outlets also struck for a $15 per hour minimum wage, sometimes with and sometimes without union backing. This "Fight for $15" movement has gradually won its demands in many cities and some states. Nurses struck in hospitals across the country in 2018, and their struggle continues.

Thousands of prisoners also staged strikes in many "correctional institutions" in 2018, emphasizing their super-exploited status as workers in the prison industrial complex, commemorating the historic Attica rebellion of 1971 and the heroic leadership of George Jackson, who was murdered in August 1971.

The case of Mumia Abu Jamal, the former Black Panther and journalist falsely convicted of murder in the death of a Philadelphia cop in 1981, has been especially important. Keeping Mumia alive, and fighting for his freedom, has been central to revolutionary work for nearly four decades. Mountains of evidence have proved him innocent of murder, but he was sentenced to death. Appeals, legal motions, millions of petition signatures, and endless street mobilizations forced his death penalty to be voided. And in late 2018, more new evidence gave hope of overturning his conviction. The Fraternal Order of Police is determined to kill him. His millions of supporters are just as determined to free him.

Leonard Peltier's case is similar. A leader of the American Indian Movement's legendary 1975 battle with the FBI at Pine Ridge Indian Reservation, Leonard was convicted of the murder of two FBI special agents, despite evidence of his innocence. His supporters have mounted a non-stop campaign for his freedom for the past four-plus decades, including a yearly "Day of Mourning" rally at Plymouth Rock as an alternative to the American Thanksgiving feast.

Fighting for Puerto Rico's independence from U.S. colonialism is another permanent part of revolutionary work. Since a U.S. president responded to a hurricane disaster there by throwing a roll of paper towels to the victims, Puerto Ricans have become more and more ready to fight back, both stateside and on the island. Puerto Ricans have won the right to full citizenship status, but also have the right to independence and self-determination.

These virtually permanent struggles are like the tide. They may recede at times, but they inevitably surge forth again and again. Meanwhile, some Puerto Ricans, like Alexandria Ocasio-Cortez, make many of us hope they'll stay, and help lead the revolution! AOC and many others are focusing on saving the planet and ushering in a Green New Deal. That in turn, I believe, could usher in the revolution we need.

Most important, we must realize that the giant fossil fuel companies, big pharma, the banks and insurance companies, and all the others in the military-industrial complex will fight tooth and nail against the Green New Deal. Even if it is the only way to save this country and the world from climate disaster – and *extinction* – the owners of these capitalist monsters know *they* will be extinct if we win a Green New Deal. Does this mean we should be pessimistic and not fight for it? AOC doesn't think so; she calls it a moral imperative. I do too. I believe we need to match her fearlessness, and mobilize aggressively to bring on the revolution. But we need to prepare for the fight of the century – or of the millennium.

Reflections:

I admire AOC's fearlessness, but she isn't perfect. She has made significant mistakes, especially on foreign policy issues. For example, when Trump ridiculed socialism in his January 2019 "state of the union" address by pointing to Venezuela, she lamely declared it's "an issue of authoritarian regime versus democracy." Rightwingers loved it. Fox News pounced on it. AOC had fallen into a trap – using the language of imperialism.

Stan Goff, a fellow DSA member and author of numerous books including *Hideous Dream* and *Full Spectrum Disorder*, wrote AOC an open letter: "I realize you are swimming in the swift currents of national politics, and you can't be expected to research everything... I admit that it's tough to tell the truth about Venezuela when the US ruling class has so effectively muddied the water, but that is what real leaders do. Discover the truth and tell it, even if you will be swimming in yet deeper, swifter waters. You are a leader now, a powerfully influential one, and that's why I'm asking you to distinguish reality from propaganda..."

Goff continued: "I know we all make these kinds of mistakes. Yours have impact. This statement about Venezuela is a mistake. A big one..." Stan proceeded to give AOC a lesson about neo-liberalism: "you may not have studied its history in Venezuela. Henceforth, please study the history of neoliberalism in any other country before you say things you hear from MSNBC — a neoliberal news outlet that is a fully owned subsidiary of the Democratic Party neoliberal establishment."

He concluded the open letter saying "We all make mistakes. The best of us admit them, learn from them, and move on to make new mistakes. The struggle you and I are in together in the U.S. is the same one as those Venezuelans who have invested their hope in the Bolivarian project, warts and all. We are the global anti-austerity movement, the fight against neoliberalism.

"With great respect and my continued support, Stan"

A few months later AOC co-signed a letter "to express our deep concern regarding the Trump Administration's handling of relations with Venezuela, particularly its suggestions of military intervention, imposition of broad unilateral sanctions, and recent recognition of an opposition leader as interim president..." They warned that sanctions could "exacerbate the country's grave economic crisis, causing immense suffering for the most vulnerable in society who bear no responsibility for the situation." But they couldn't stop there; going on to "strongly condemn" Venezuelan President Maduro for repression, economic failure, "illegitimate elections," and "blocking" aid.

There's that trap again. Join the chorus, blame the victim of U.S. strangulation, distort the truth, be acceptable to the caucus.

Washington, DC, of course, is a poisonous cesspool of racist, imperialist power mongering. Anyone breathing the air there can be infected by it – even

AOC. I continue to appreciate her invaluable contributions to the popular struggle for socialism and justice. And I hope she accepts Stan Goff's advice to "study the history of neoliberalism in any other country before you say things" that hurt the interests of peace and justice. We need her to heed that advice.

AOC is even worse on China, calling for sanctions, denouncing "China's gross human rights abuses" in Tibet, hailing "pro-democracy direct actions" in Hong Kong, and so on. AOC's squad partner Ilhan Omar spoke better – but still not good enough: "We need to distinguish between justified criticisms of the Chinese government's human rights record and a Cold War mentality that uses China as a scapegoat for our own domestic problems and demonizes Chinese Americans."

Only new squad member Jamaal Bowman managed to steer clear of cold war chatter: "I strongly reject any anti-China rhetoric..., and we must be vigilant about the impacts of such rhetoric on AAPI communities at a time of increased hate crimes." Bowman added that "We won't be able to solve the challenges of the 21st century like the climate crisis and global health unless we have relationships that harness partnerships across the globe, including China."

The toxic climate in Washington makes it hard to stay clear on the nature of the arguments. That's why leftists must continually press the squad and other progressives in Congress to tell the truth, and not fall victim to poisonous political propaganda that pollutes the DC air.

14 – Messages from the Future

How could things turn out if the Green New Deal were to succeed? To help imagine it, in mid-April 2019, Alexandria Ocasio-Cortez teamed up with Naomi Klein, illustrator Molly Crabapple and *The Intercept* to present a futuristic cartoon-art video scenario.

They realized, Klein wrote, that "the biggest obstacle to the kind of transformative change the Green New Deal envisions is overcoming the skepticism that humanity could ever pull off something at this scale and speed... The idea that societies could collectively decide to embrace rapid foundational changes to transportation, housing, energy, agriculture, forestry, and more — precisely what is needed to avert climate breakdown — is not something for which most of us have any living reference. *We have grown up bombarded with the message that there is no alternative to the crappy system that is destabilizing the planet and hoarding vast wealth at the top.*" [Emphasis added.]

AOC says the first big step is "just closing our eyes and imagining it... We can be whatever we have the courage to see," adding that the Green New Deal "is our plan for a future worth fighting for." It reminds me of another message from the future, John Lennon's *Imagine*, released in 1988:

> *You may say that I'm a dreamer*
> *But I'm not the only one*
> *I hope someday you'll join us*
> *And the world will live as one.*

What if we imagine we can change everything? Imagine no more prisons – it isn't hard to do. Imagine all the people living life in peace! Imagine free medical care, free 24-hour child care, free tuition for as long as you want to study. Free transportation. Free *time!* (like "Somewhere" from *Westside Story*) Imagine good housing for everyone.

Imagine lots of interesting and challenging work to do – jobs converting homes, schools and businesses for solar energy. Engineers and construction workers would be in high demand for all types of conversion work – building the new super-grid to carry wind, water, thermal and solar power across the country and around the world. We'll need to upgrade thousands of miles of rail for new bullet trains. Many more teachers will be needed, since we could reduce class sizes by a lot. Imagine favorite things and "least favorites" – much better food available at affordable prices; many fewer cops, judges, courts and jails. On and on.

In the video AOC says, looking back from the future, "People were scared. They said it was too big, too fast, not practical. I think that's because they just couldn't picture it yet." It recalls FDR declaring "the only thing we have to fear is fear itself."

People are afraid, of course – of cops bashing their heads, killing or kidnapping their children and throwing them in jail, of losing their jobs and their homes, whatever scraps and leftovers they have held onto while losing continuously. Many also fear to dream of new possibilities. They have heard repeatedly that "socialism can never work." This fear can be paralyzing.

Occupy Wall Street did the same. So did the 1934 long-shore workers' general strike in San Francisco, and the 1937 sit-down strikes in the auto industry.

All these victorious upsurges shared a common characteristic: a determination that if we dare to fight, we can win!

But they didn't go far enough. The beauty of the Green New Deal is its resolution to *change everything*. There's a recognition that to transform our economy to renewable energy we must harness and mobilize *people power*, and demobilize corporate power. There's a fearless determination to transform government itself, by having working people *take over*.

AOC looks back on a victory for government-funded elections – no more corporate money to rig elections and buy votes in Congress. She doesn't mention changing the Constitution, but we can imagine that protecting private property interests will no longer be the top priority.

"Twelve years to change everything," AOC says. "How we got around, how we fed ourselves, how we made our stuff, how we lived and worked — *everything*. The only way to do it was to transform our economy, which we already knew was broken."

Some of us have been working for this future for decades. Five decades may seem like a long time, but it has passed in a blur for me. Like many of my generation, who were jolted awake by the Vietnam war and the civil rights movement, I thought change would come sooner and be easier. We didn't fully understand the tenacity of the system. We didn't pay much attention to what Marx advised 150 years ago: capitalism is resilient, and will hang on until all its possibilities are exhausted; capitalists and their politicians will blush at nothing to keep their power intact.

In 1969 Nixon escalated *COINTELPRO* (first used in the witch hunt of the 1950s) to crush the Black liberation movement. Legality was not an issue in this massive terror campaign in the name of "law and order," designed to wipe out the Black Panther Party and all other outcroppings of revolutionary Black leadership. Then Reagan launched the drug war, which was really a renewal of the Jim Crow system that had operated for most of the century to keep African-American people "in their place." Now, after about four decades of mass incarceration, the drug war has lost credibility. But its brutal toll continues.

Police kill Black people simply for "walking while Black." At least 2.2 million people are currently held in U.S. federal, state and local jails. About 465,000 are in "pre-trial detention." This last category would logically be considered very short-term, but in fact holding times often stretch out for years, exposing prisoners to extremely brutal, even fatal conditions. Another 840,000 people are on parole, and a staggering 3.7 million people are on probation. [17] Marked as pariahs, they effectively are imprisoned on the street. The prison population shot up by more than 900 percent from 1980 to 2018.

But as the saying goes, you can jail or kill revolutionaries, but you really can't stop revolution. It's the force of life itself. The Black Lives Matter movement has emerged and surged in response to all the police killings and mass incarceration. And it is linking with such movements as Fight for 15 – a movement for a new minimum wage – sanctuary for immigrants, and others. The Lesbian, Gay, Bisexual, and Transsexual (LGBTQ) liberation movement is also a key factor. *All* oppressed people naturally fight for their rights and freedom. Those who have been oppressed the longest generally fight the hardest. And, of course, the more freedom we fight for, the more we will win.

Most of this was not obvious to me in 1968. It took five decades of living struggle and learning to "get it." There is still much to learn. In a sense, the resilience of capitalism and the reactionaries forces us to learn more. Take Cuba for example. In the early days of the revolution, the old traditional patriarchal patterns remained more or less intact. But over the years the Cuban leadership came to understand that gay liberation was part of the revolution. In recent years, educational campaigns on LGBTQ issues have been implemented under the leadership of Mariela Castro, Raúl's daughter.

---

[17] https://www.prisonpolicy.org/reports/pie2018.html

This has helped the LGBTQ movement in the U.S. and worldwide start to realize that socialism and liberation really go together.

Today's movement remains focused on resistance – just as I was 50 years ago. But I think the direction is clear. Once you start resisting, you end up going for revolution. Now, with the Green New Deal resolution *mushrooming* into a massive and urgent movement, and Black Lives Matter refusing to step back, revolution can become the order of the day.

The extreme inequality in U.S. society, and the brutality waged constantly against people of color and immigrants, as well as the threat that reckless capitalism might actually destroy the planet – all of these outrages create a buildup of pressure that will explode eventually. Over the past two decades there have been hints, like when Trump and Sessions began grabbing small children from their parents and throwing both the kids and the parents in *separate* jails, millions of people protested in a variety of ways. The government was forced to pull back, at least briefly. White supremacists who in August 2017 had staged an openly fascist rally in Charlottesville, VA, killing one anti-fascist and injuring many others, were stopped in their tracks a year later when they tried to mobilize again. That's a sign of growing strength on "our side."

In recent years I have focused on the issues of affordable housing and homelessness. In the richest country on the planet nearly half of renters can't afford rent, and millions are home-less. Rent hikes and reduced household income are major causes of homelessness, along with falling wages. Tenant harassment by profit-gouging landlords is a key factor. A fashionable solution is to provide a percentage of "affordable" rental units in new market-rate *(ie, luxury)* buildings. Imagine instead a massive construction drive to build good, clean, affordable and sustainable housing for everyone.

Housing is not considered a right in the USA, in spite of the Universal Declaration of Human Rights (Article 25). The only *guaranteed right,* in terms of housing, is payment of rent or mortgage. If you fall behind you're out on the street. Detroit enjoyed decades of boom when the "big three" auto makers reigned supreme globally, but then lost a million residents between 1970 and 2010, shrinking from about 1.7 million people to about 700,000. Most of the displaced people were African-American workers and their families, who had migrated from the South to take jobs in the auto industry. A huge number of these people lost their homes to foreclosure when they couldn't meet their mortgage payments during the crash of 2008.

Healthcare is also not considered a right in the USA – the only industrialized country without universal healthcare. Profit-oriented medicine is a national disaster, but the drug and insurance companies – and the politicians they fund – refuse to have it any other way. Meanwhile more people die each year from opioid overdoses (75,000) than from auto accidents. This epidemic seems largely to be about depression from job losses and despair. Overall, the suicide rate has increased by over 50 percent since 1980. Suicides among military veterans averaged *20 per day* between 1979 and 2014. The COVID19 crisis has made the private health care system not merely a disaster, but an obvious crime against humanity.

Add these disasters to the utter failure of U.S. education – a virtual apartheid system – in which a large percentage of students finish primary and secondary school unable to read or write, and an ever larger share of college graduates cannot find jobs while finding themselves saddled with a lifetime of debt.

The explosive pressure is intensifying. Today more people in the USA favor socialism than capitalism according to polls. No wonder! It gets easier and easier to hate capitalism. Right-wingers denounce universal healthcare and other basic rights as "creeping socialism." But now people are saying, "If that's socialism, that's what I want!"

Women were especially strong against Trump from inauguration day onward. Their role in opposing the outrageous nomination of sex offender Kavanaugh to the Supreme Court was especially significant. I believe we have only seen the beginning. Women have historically been decisive in successful revolutions. They started it in Russia in February 1917; they were crucial participants in Vietnam's liberation, and in China's transformation. The *#MeToo!* movement has brought disgrace on and ruined the careers of significant numbers of top executives. Take AOC herself, and the new generation of insurgents in Congress. They're signs of the times, and there will surely be others who will win in other states and cities around the country.

We can't topple the system through elections alone, but it's a start. These victories definitely weaken the corrupt, bureaucratic, patriarchal power structure. And they are a harbinger of the future.

In 2010, the Occupy Wall Street movement seemed to emerge out of nowhere, and electrified the country by denouncing the savage inequality of capitalism. No permanent damage, perhaps, but on the west coast some occupiers aligned themselves with the militant International Longshore

Union, shutting down shipping from Seattle to San Diego for several days. Again, no permanent damage, but a clear signal: united we can shut down this monstrous system.

This is a miracle that could happen – it just takes a little longer than merely running for socialism in elections. Electing some socialists will help, but we'll need more, which brings us back to the GI resistance. As John Catalinotto explains in his excellent book, *Turn the Guns Around*, there is direct linkage historically between mutinies, soldier revolts, and revolutions.

If the soldiers refuse to fight but keep their weapons, that could put the government in a bind. If other sectors of society rebel at the same time, we could have a situation of "dual power" – people's power *vs* the power of the state. At that point revolution could be the solution, especially if the economy is in crisis and the government has lost wars around the world and credibility at home. At that point it becomes a question of revolutionary leadership, unity and determination.

Trump is gone now, but his foreign policy lives on: sanctions against any country that wants its own path. U.S. foreign policy is like a gigantic game of "chicken" – counting on the other guys to chicken out first. "The other guys" currently include many of the traditional allies of the USA, other imperialist countries that have been reliable partners in exploiting and confronting the rest of the world. Canadians and Europeans are not so anxious to go along with sanctions against Iran, or to stop trading with China. In fact *they depend on China* to help shore up their shaky economies. How ironic! The power of China's mixed economy – which is anchored by strong central planning and a very strong centralized banking system – is emerging as a kind of "savior" for capitalist economies across the globe. Its Belt and Road initiative has received a warm welcome far and wide, despite U.S. denunciations. In Africa, China presents an alternate development model that is vastly more attractive than the debt trap imposed by the U.S.-sponsored World Bank and Inter-national Monetary Fund.

China and Russia have forged strong economic ties with Iran and Venezuela, frustrating U.S. efforts to isolate, strangle or invade them. Sanctions – *i.e.,* economic siege warfare – and military threats are the current U.S. weapons of choice to isolate and bludgeon such countries. And there is always the danger that the U.S. will lash out in anger and frustration, launching a desperate hot war against any or all of these countries. But the U.S. military is so bogged down in central Asia and the Middle East that it looks more and more like a helpless giant.

The USA has been waging war against China ever since the revolution of 1949 – either openly or by proxy. The so-called "UN police action" in Korea reached the Chinese border in 1952, and was pushed back decisively by Chinese Red Army forces. Even the U.S. war against Vietnam can be seen as a brazen threat to China. But the U.S. was defeated by the Vietnamese liberation forces, with support from both China and the USSR.

One legacy of the massive resistance to the U.S. war against Vietnam is that the U.S. has had to use military contractors with thousands of expensive mercenaries (instead of conscripted soldiers) to wage endless and unwinnable wars in Iraq and Afghanistan. The main reason young people in this country don a military uniform today is to have a job. But they come home disillusioned, at best. The government can't really get recruits to actually *believe* in their imperialist mission. And military resistance continues and grows. *(See Appendix 7.)*

I'm reminded of an old slogan: *What if they held a war and nobody came?* The Green New Deal could even make that happen. Eliminate the need for oil and a major cause of war disappears. If there are lots of jobs for young people, they won't want to choose the military, which will have to shrink drastically anyway. The only "war" to fight will be against die-hard capitalists desperately determined to hold on to their old system. This will surely be rough at first. But massive, large-scale mobilization to convert the economy and change society can literally *change everything* – including the death grip of the old system on the minds of people.

Overcoming fear can happen. AOC suggests that people's confidence will build as new things happen. Small victories will pile on each other to generate a crescendo of new possibilities. We have to get organized, and start the process.

People will feel the need to fight back, but will need help and leadership to mobilize effectively. We can thank Bernie Sanders, AOC, and others for inspiring today's surge toward socialism. But we must hope and struggle for a serious commitment to unification within the progressive movement. My hope and vision is that popular movements will force this unification, as they start to merge into larger coalitions of resistance. But I worry. Can we do it fast enough to forestall the emergence of fascist forces that know how to take advantage of the situation?

In the coming years we need a gigantic people's movement, organized at every level: in neighborhoods, work places, and councils of many kinds. We need *transition councils* where delegates from neighborhoods and workplaces deliberate about how to organize recovery from the pandemic, and how to take over metropolitan and regional power authorities. They could institute monitoring operations to call out corruption and police brutality; launch cooperative ventures for home building and conversion, as well as innovative food distribution. These cooperatives could then demand funding for local conversion efforts, instead of waiting for the government or the private sector to deliver renewable power.

People's councils could become incubators of a new people's democracy. Local, regional, sectoral and national people's councils might function as a new power, gradually growing strong enough either to challenge or to check the power of traditional representative bodies.

These are just possibilities. Ideas to imagine. The main thing is to imagine that the people – that is, the working people – can take on the job of running the country. There will surely be mistakes and failed experiments. But one thing seems certain. We can do it better than the current gang of robbers and opportunists. We just need the courage and organization to go for it.

14 – The Stakes and the Odds

When Scott Walker became Governor of Wisconsin in 2011, he was funded lavishly by the Koch brothers. Their father was a founder of the super-racist and anti-union John Birch Society. Walker's first move was to crush the public sector unions. A massive popular occupation of Wisconsin's capitol rotunda in Madison followed, which threatened to become a general strike. But union leaders backed down, opting instead for the next election. Two elections later, Walker was finally defeated, but still fights on. Meanwhile the U.S. Supreme Court ruled in 2018 that public sector workers do *not* have the right to strike. This followed Koch-funded campaigns to get super-rightist judges on the court. But the court is not the final arbiter – the fight in the streets will decide. And the "red for ed" marches of teachers in "red states" have been decisive so far. ("Red" is now, ironically, the iconic color of Republicans. But when the teachers wear red T-shirts, they return the color to its true origins.)

After the collapse of the USSR, some pundits in the early 1990s declared "the end of history" – suggesting that the end of the Cold War had brought the end of competition between capitalism and any alternatives, the end of the class struggle. The loss of the USSR did cause confusion and disarray on the left, and emboldened the capitalists. But the struggle continues. Now there's a "pivot to Asia," with U.S. carrier battle groups trolling the South China Sea, THAAD missiles deployed in South Korea and Okinawa, endless wars in central Asia and the Middle East, and more than 800 U.S. military bases around the world. There is a battle for Africa, with the U.S. rushing to catch up with Chinese development projects there, and setting up "counter-terrorist" operations across that vast continent. U.S. sanctions wage a siege against Iran, Venezuela, Nicaragua, Russia, China, and any other country that takes an independent road. All of these efforts at strangulation amount to acts of war.

Young American soldiers are deployed to all these "hot spots" without really knowing why they are there or what they should do about it. My suggestion is they should resist – refuse illegal orders, not allow themselves to be pawns of a brazen but failing imperialism.

Why must there be wars and U.S. bases everywhere? Because U.S. capitalism needs to control all the markets – it must expand or die. The same is true on the home front. Rightwing politicians and pundits oppose anything that seems socialist, like the Green New Deal, free universal health care, free education, government subsidies for the poor, even public transportation. Why? For them, anything that interferes with the "free market" is bad for the economy. The real reason may be less theoretical. Major beneficiaries of private health care are giant insurance and pharmaceutical companies. In education, privatization is rampant and growing. Why? Perhaps profits are needed anywhere they can be made available – a sign of a weak and desperate economic system.

So a new question arises. *Does capitalism work?* If the success criterion is a system's ability to provide for *all* the people who live in the system, the answer must be negative. So why does the system continue? An ever growing percentage of the U.S. public budget is for the military, the police and the judicial system. Another large portion is reserved to bolster the big banks, and other major businesses that fund the politicians who "regulate" them. The military budget guarantees control of oil resources around the world by U.S. corporations. Countries that don't cooperate are strangled, like Venezuela today. U.S. military and intelligence resources also work 24/7/365 to bolster client governments and destabilize any that stray towards independence.

Capitalism fails often. The Great Depression of the 1930s was one example. But we have since had black Fridays, stormy Mondays, massive market failures in Asia and Latin America, and the "Great Recession" of 2008 – from which the so-called "recovery" has been largely an illusion. Now we have a pandemic, which has demonstrated the utter incapacity of capitalist leaders to manage the crisis and avoid massive loss of lives.

During the Great Recession, only China's dynamism served as a lifeline for the global system – ironically, since it was China's strategically mixed economy, based on central planning and a strong state sector combined with "reform and opening up" to both local and international capitalist investors, that was the secret of success. In the decade following the 2008 crash, while infrastructure in Europe and the U.S. was crumbling, and neither public nor private investment could be mobilized to fix the problem and stimulate the faltering economies, China built new metropolitan transportation systems in more than two dozen cities, together with a network of intercity "bullet trains," plus highways, bridges, hydroelectric dams, and so on. In the process, China has eliminated extreme poverty for more than 800 million people.

During the COVID19 pandemic, China's leaders mobilized at lightning speed to save the country. The contrast between what happened in China and in the USA was stark enough to make a lot of people wake up. That didn't stop Trump and Pompeo from blaming China for the pandemic, but most people did not go along with that nonsense.

China's economy is now the second largest in the world, and in purchasing power parity is actually larger than the U.S. economy. China is making a bid to lead a major share of other countries. U.S. efforts to isolate Iran, for example, are unlikely to succeed, since China buys a substantial percentage of Iran's oil. In fact, the USA is isolating itself – dangerous, of course, given its continued military might. But this country is so massively over-extended and ineffectual that U.S. threats may not materialize. Regarding China's mixed economy, while some leftists despair of a "transition to capitalism," I think the strong centralization of the economy, and leadership by the 90-million-strong Communist Party, are significant anchors.

For contrast, let's look at the Great Depression of the 1930s, when millions of people in the U.S. and around the world lost their jobs, and often their homes, because a speculative frenzy by Wall Street went bad. The underlying reason was a "crisis of over-production" – the system was producing more goods than could be sold at a profit. Something was needed to stimulate more buying. Since people were out of work, they couldn't buy what they needed. The U.S. president of the time, Franklin Roosevelt (FDR), instituted some quasi-socialist measures to save the situation, including public works on large scale infrastructure projects, Social Security, a minimum wage, and union rights. It wasn't enough, but rightists fought him every step, denouncing these measures as "creeping socialism." It took a war – World

War 2 – to generate sufficient demand to get the system running again. Huge contracts for guns, tanks, uniforms, war ships, bombers, and so on created the demand the capitalists needed to once again produce at a profit.

This war economy has continued ever since. The U.S. capitalist economy is now totally dependent on the military sector, which dominates all other sectors with disastrous results. "Guns and butter" used to be considered realistic, but now government policy makers and rightist politicians regularly say "we can't afford" virtually all non-military public needs. As a result the U.S. quality of life gets worse and worse, with more and more young people looking at a lifetime of debt for higher education, weird and uncertain job prospects in the so-called "gig economy," or joining the military or ending up in jail.

I did not have to pay tuition when I went to college in the 1960s, and consider it an outrage that young people are denied that opportunity today. Now the U.S. education system is no longer merely in crisis; it's a failure. When I taught in New York's public schools, I discovered that a significant percentage of the students were functionally illiterate. In the South Bronx, these students are part of the infamous "school-to-prison pipeline." Many face the grim choice of military service or a street life that ultimately leads either to self-destruction or prison. Many people blame the kids, but a society that cannot offer a realistic future to its young people has failed.

This failure is a hard pill to swallow for many white members of my generation, who grew up in prosperity. After WW2 the U.S. was the big winner in both Europe and Asia, emerging as the dominant economy in the post-war period, with endless markets for profitable investment across the globe. Now this dominance is fraying, which has led to continuous economic uncertainty, and ever riskier investment strategies. War and threats of war are now constant, but the ability of the U.S. to actually win wars has diminished drastically. The cynicism is overwhelming, and my personal hope is that more and more young people will simply refuse to be used as cannon fodder.

The end of WW2 also led to the "Cold War" between capitalism and socialism. I grew up during this period, some-times wondering what made the Soviet Union so bad, and often thinking the "Cold War" wasn't really so cold. The Soviet Union was the other major winner in WW2 – successfully resisting and defeating a Nazi invasion at a cost of more than 20 million lives. The Red Army occupied the countries of eastern Europe while U.S. and allied troops rushed to occupy as much of defeated Germany as possible, to deny this prize to the socialist regime. That was the second time capitalism had "saved" Germany from socialism. A fierce counter-revolution in the 1920s prevented a workers' victory there at that time, which would have made a healthier European socialist commonwealth possible. U.S. military and economic efforts in France and Italy also staved off socialist possibilities in those two countries after WW2. The Soviet Union was too weakened by the war's devastation to provide support, and was focused on rebuilding and defense. So golden opportunities were lost. But the war had devastated the old European colonial system, opening possibilities for independence and self-determination in the former colonies in Africa and Asia.

The defeat of Japanese imperialism at the end of WW2 was a combined (but not allied) achievement of the USA and the communist movement. The Chinese communists fought a brutal occupation of their country by Japan that led to successful revolution in 1949. In Vietnam, the national liberation forces led by Ho Chi Minh and the Vietnamese communists kicked out the Japanese and declared indepen-dence in 1945, only to have their former French colonial masters try to stage a comeback, with U.S. support. In Korea, the communists took over as the Japanese occupiers retreated, but the U.S. military intervened, hoping not only to push back the communists in Korea, but to use the Korean peninsula as a base to attack and destroy the Chinese revolution.

In 2019 people across the globe looked on anxiously as South Korea's liberal President Moon tried to achieve the impossible, getting to peace between the USA and North Korea. North Korea's leader, Kim Jong Un, proved capable of stout resistance to bullying by the crazy man in Washington, who seemed to think China would help pressure Kim. But Chinese leaders remember too much. The so-called "UN Police Action" in Korea ended in an "armistice" in 1953, but all U.S. administrations since that time have refused to sign a peace treaty, and have maintained a U.S. military occupation there, with 28,000+ troops backed up by THAAD "anti-missile" systems and other heavy war gear – plus even more in nearby Okinawa. It is an open secret that this occupation is not only aimed at North Korea, but also China, as well as Russia, just as the original war in Korea was. At that time, anti-war writer I.F. Stone's *Hidden History of the Korean War* exposed that U.S. commanders carried the war to the Chinese border, where they were met by the Chinese People's Army, which turned them back sharply. The infamous General Douglas MacArthur was held responsible, and was ultimately fired by President Truman for insubordination. Interestingly, he became much more popular than Truman – the public and the media seemed to like his war mongering.

As socialists in the homeland of imperialism, we don't just look on anxiously – we *mobilize*. Whether on a picket line of a dozen people or a thundering march and rally, we view it as our internationalist duty – and our *patriotic duty* – to mobilize to stop the warmakers. Yes, *patriotic!* Over time, more and more people will get it: the warmakers are *not* patriotic – *we are!* If we can build some harmony between the people of the USA and the people of the rest of the world, that could save us all. The harmony we want is based on solidarity. In the current period that must be *anti-imperialist* solidarity, because imperialism is a crime against humanity. We know we'll need to bring down the criminals in Washington, and their Wall Street backers, to make this happen, but that will definitely make the world a better place!

In 2002 and 2003, there was a crescendo of ever larger mass protests aimed at George W. Bush's war buildup against Iraq. It started in October 2002, right after Bush signed his war authorization. More than 100,000 protested in Washington. Millions more marched all over the world, and by mid-February the millions of protesters in streets everywhere stimulated a New York Times front-page report to say "there are two superpowers on the planet: the United States and worldwide public opinion."

We cannot yet claim "superpower" status against imperial-ism. Bush dismissed these protests as a few "interest groups." His "endless war" adventures have been discredited, even though they remain endless. Our mobilizations have not been able to stop them *yet*.

As of 2020 there were active U.S. wars in Afghanistan, Iraq and Syria, a "balance of terror" on the Korean peninsula, a massive escalation of military threats against Iran and China, proxy wars and siege warfare against Venezuela and Nicaragua, war games across Africa, and more than 800 U.S. military bases around the world. All this has a single purpose: to maintain U.S. domination in an unequal world. Like Martin Luther King, Jr., "I refuse to accept the view that mankind is so tragically bound to the starless midnight of racism and war that the bright daybreak of peace and brotherhood can never become a reality..." But I also know that "Human progress is neither automatic nor inevitable... Every step toward the goal of justice requires sacrifice, suffering, and struggle; the tireless exertions and passionate concern of dedicated individuals."

Now, with a 12-year "deadline" to avoid human extinction, the stakes have become higher. We face an emergency, which may be enough to make very large numbers of people take action. That improves the odds of winning – that is, of trans-forming human society and saving the planet – but time is short.

There remains a question about whether capitalism or socialism is more "democratic." It may seem obvious when the constant distortions and violations of democracy by U.S. leaders are considered. Nixon's Watergate break-ins were just a hint: he and his backers would do *anything* to win. While he was forced to resign in disgrace, even the opponents of his lurch toward dictatorship rallied around his hand-picked successors to rescue their system. And when George W. Bush stole the 2000 election, the Supreme Court ratified it. Ten years later in 2010 the Supreme Court ratified *Citizens United*, granting "free speech" to corporations as "persons," meaning they could spend limitless funds on their preferred candidates, so money is the determining factor in "democratic" elections.

Despite all this, the mainstream media maintains that any and all socialist experiments are hopeless dictatorships, doomed to fail. And they cheer on the government as it does everything possible to suppress any chance of success for socialist experiments anywhere and everywhere.

Reflections:
"Swimming against the tide" is an acquired discipline and art. Salmon expend their life energy returning from the sea to their birthplaces high in the source waters of the Columbia River and other fierce northwestern streams. Nothing can stop them from leaping against the current to complete their destiny. That same tenacity is required for revolutionaries.

15 – Up From the Ashes: Reflections on the Pandemic

When I was in Nicaragua during the first Sandinista decade (the 1980s), there was a saying: *No hay mal que por bien no venga:* there's no bad thing that doesn't bring some good. It has been a useful reminder as the country and the world slid into catastrophe with the COVID19 pandemic. My whirlwind started in the 1960s, with rebellion against the U.S. war in Vietnam and the racist violence at home. This time the wind has been stronger, and more dangerous in many ways.

The pandemic has changed everything. Trump's ineptness and buffoonish bluster caused countless deaths and endangered everyone. The system was out of control. But people began to fight back.

Solidarity made a comeback. Some was real, like "free fridges" that sprang up on the streets in cities across the country. And then there's the congressional version. In spring 2020, money by the *trillions* flooded to banks and big business; for ordinary people, there was about enough to cover rent for a month or two, plus some unemployment checks. Landlords had to put evictions on hold in some places.

Some of the government's generosity raised questions: Trump suggested eliminating payroll taxes during the pandemic. Nice idea, but a major part of the payroll tax is the 15 percent of gross that workers pay into Social Security, which is matched by the employer. Was this meant as a "trojan horse" to get rid of Social Security, or just a clever way to take several months of payments away from future retirees?

There was plenty of corruption and profit gouging – some in Congress made a bundle by selling stocks based on what they knew before anyone else. Profiteers hauled in windfalls by selling essential supplies that should have been provided by the government. Trump tried to buy out a German vaccine maker, so the vaccine could become a U.S. monopoly, but his offer was rejected. Meanwhile, for big corporations, the bailout has been a bonanza – untold trillions to save the system.

Common people have banded together for mutual support and common demands. There is a new stage of the "political revolution" Bernie Sanders launched. At the start of the pandemic Sanders won the best unemployment package ever: coverage for *all* people who needed it – "independent con-tractors," restaurant workers and gig workers – at a higher rate. This briefly changed the Congressional agenda, prioritizing basic survival. Sanders argued for a recovery focused on the Green New Deal.

The scope and depth of the crisis was unprecedented. The numbers of people out of work skyrocketed to millions. Trump panicked, calling for everyone to get back to work "by Easter" – a nice pander to his evangelical base. But the natural laws of capitalism don't depend on miracles. Supply follows demand. Even though 20th century capitalism succeeded in "manufacturing" demand, this time it would take bigger miracles. Putting money into people's pockets would allow them to buy groceries and medication for a while, but the survival of the system depends on a vast global market, and the pandemic has paralyzed populations and markets across the globe. People's health and safety have really come first, for the first time ever in most countries. But people have had to fight for their health and safety. Trump backpedaled his "back to work suggestion" as essential services workers threatened to strike.

The crisis showed how massive debt has crippled the lives of ordinary people – mortgage debt, medical debt, car debt, student debt, credit card debt, payday loan debts, and personal debt. Instead of life savings people could fall back on, millions face overwhelming, unpayable debt. A mass movement has emerged to cancel the debt: "We can't pay, we *won't* pay!"

As money flooded out to save the system and provide bandaids, it raised questions: if all that money is there in a crisis, if it's possible to have a moratorium on student debt, why not *cancel* the debt? If transit can be free in a crisis, *why not all the time?* If prisoners can be released in a crisis (as they were in some cities), why not *free them all,* permanently? If the government can flood the system with money, *why does anyone have to be homeless?*

The social and economic breakdown has set off a social and political break*through:* people have stopped waiting, and are mobilizing to end the suffering. People power has begun to grow as the empire weakens. Trump's mismanagement shredded his vaunted invincibility. His efforts to blame the coronavirus on China fizzled, as China's effective "people's war" against the virus impressed people everywhere. Trump insisted on calling COVID19 "the China virus." Asian people across the country often paid the price, as racist incidents proliferated. There have been solidarity efforts in defense of Asians, but not enough.

While Trump and his Secretary of State Pompeo intensified sanctions against Iran and Venezuela – hoping to strangle them as the pandemic raged – Chinese medical workers and supplies came to the rescue in those countries, in Europe, and elsewhere. Cuban doctors and Cuban medication joined them.

But Trump and Pompeo continued to beat war drums. In March 2020, European NATO members cancelled participation in planned war games against Russia. As U.S. global prestige shrank, European leaders also found ways to get around U.S. sanctions against Iran, because the U.S. banking system seemed less threatening than before.

Reports that government planners, together with big pharma, had conducted detailed simulations of the pandemic months before it broke out raised questions: *Why weren't they prepared? Why didn't their planning result in stockpiles of needed supplies? What was the purpose of their planning? Was it just to help big pharma cash in?*

The glaring inadequacies of the U.S. healthcare system have made the demand for Medicare for All even more urgent.

At home, the crisis generated more popular mobilization, not less. "We need to build a political revolution not just to make the Green New Deal victorious in this election, but to upend the balance of power in this country for a generation," said Dyanna Jaye, the Sunrise Movement's organizing director. The campaign to change America has really only begun. Varshini Prakash of Sunrise declared, "Our movement is more powerful than ever, but we are in a fight for the soul of this country… We know that no matter what happens over the coming months, elections alone won't be enough… That's why our movement is oriented around a guiding strategy for this year of: *Organize, Vote, and Strike.*" She meant student strikes, but with schools shuttered, the youth supported and joined in *rent strikes* in many cities, as well as refusals to work without protective gear and hazard pay by nurses and other essential services workers. And a people's strike movement emerged, fueled by walkouts of Black workers in scores of occupations, including longshore workers on both coasts, as well as wildcats at Amazon and auto factories.

"History has shown that when millions of young people dedicate themselves to a cause, and show up in overwhelming numbers, revolutionary change isn't just possible — it's inevitable," Prakash declared. "As long as we are organizing our generation into an unstoppable force in American politics, we will eventually ensure that the Green New Deal comes to pass — no matter what happens this election."

The Sunrise Movement appeared almost spontaneously in early 2019, joining Alexandria Ocasio-Cortez (AOC) for a fairly polite visit to House

Speaker Nancy Pelosi's office. From there it mushroomed into a force, along with Black Lives Matter, Fight for $15, nurses, teachers, and many others.

Blanca Estevez, a DSA National Political Committee member from Arkansas, pointed to another looming force for change: the Latinx community. Bernie's outreach to Latinx voters in the 2020 Nevada primary "clinched it for him," she wrote. They also carried Bernie to victory in California, and kept him strong in Texas. Latinx people are 18% of the country's population. Together with African-Americans and other people of color, they make up more than a third of the U.S. population.

While Biden won the primary vote of African-American voters loyal to Obama, the natural working class alliance of Black and Latinx workers would be strong in the fight against Trump. This alliance includes enough other forces to be a solid majority of workers: women, men, Black, Latinx and white, LGBTQ, and immigrants of all nationalities. This is the decisive majority, together with the youth, not only for the elections, but for the future.

In 2006 there was a virtual May Day general strike in many cities, as Latinx workers banded together to make "a day without Latinx workers." An alliance of dock workers and the Occupy movement shut down ports on the West Coast in 2011.

Workers are now poised to benefit from a Green New Deal, and can be expected to fight for it – for the jobs it would bring, and for the future it could preserve for their children and grandchildren. My fantasy of millions of people joining Black Lives Matter protesting in the streets *came true!* It lasted for months, so much that Trump tried to declare war against it in the name of "law and order," which backfired against him.

Even military personnel have suffered damage, like sailors on the US aircraft carrier Theodore Roosevelt. Their captain was fired after calling for help publicly when members of the TR crew became infected. The sailors cheered him as a hero for putting their safety ahead of the "chain of command." Will other sailors and soldiers on ships and bases across the globe demand *their* safety must come first?

The question of the moment is: How can the horrifying reality here and around the world be transformed to "a future we can believe in"? The crashing economy holds the answer. The pandemic has exposed the economy's fragility and instability. Even as the Federal Reserve printed trillions of dollars to stabilize the economy and bolster Wall Street, unemployment skyrocketed to tens of millions.

The economic shudders across the globe triggered by the pandemic are a sign. In France, neoliberal President Macron's moves to change the pension system brought millions of people into the streets for a months-long general strike. Massive and repeated popular rebellions have shaken Chile, Ecuador, Haiti and Colombia. These could be seen as harbingers of a future in our country – a future that has been unfolding in the streets.

The traditional U.S. government answer to such threats has been military force, police repression, and CIA subversion. The U.S. maintains more than 800 military bases around the world, in addition to hundreds more stateside. The status quo has depended on ever more fragile economic stability, but also on effective repression and people's passivity. If soldiers and sailors themselves refuse to fight, as many did during the Vietnam era, they can disarm the military. Add to this the rest of us *becoming the whirlwind*. If we can do that by the millions, we can begin to shape a future we can believe in.

16 – *Coming: A Battle to Protect and Expand Democracy*

The lessons and impact of the 2020 elections are far reaching. The constant charges of "voter fraud" – really a campaign of attempted suppression of Black voters – harken back to the Jim Crow era that followed the post-Civil War Reconstruction period. The tactics used by the Trump campaign are a harbinger of continued stormy times ahead. And the efforts of mainstream congressional Democrats to blame the left for their disappointing results can be considered a preview of coming battles both inside and outside of the Democratic Party.

At a congressional Democratic Party caucus meeting on the Saturday after election day 2020 – while tens of thousands of Trump opponents were celebrating in the streets of cities across the country – mainstream Democrats stood up to blame progressives for costing them several important seats. Alexandria Ocasio-Cortez shot back:

"Progressive policies do not hurt candidates. Every single candidate that co-sponsored Medicare for All in a swing district kept their seat. We also know that co-sponsoring the Green New Deal was not a sinker. Mike Levin was an original co-sponsor of the legislation, and he kept his seat..."[18] Bernie Sanders echoed AOC, adding that 70 percent of voters expressed support for Medicare for All, a massive jobs program and a Green New Deal.

AOC blasted mainstream Democrats for "trying to blame the Movement for Black Lives for their loss." She highlighted the huge share of white support for Trump, who whipped up his supporters on the dangers of rioting, socialism and anarchism. AOC said "we need to do a lot of anti-racist, deep canvassing in this country." She added that "a lot of Dem strategy is... to avoid poking the bear. That's their argument with defunding police, right? To not agitate racial resentment. I don't think that is sustainable." She meant *white* racial resentment.

"I need my colleagues to understand that we are not the enemy," AOC continued. "And that their base is not the enemy. That the Movement for Black Lives is not the enemy, that Medicare for all is not the enemy... If they keep going after the wrong thing, they're just setting up their own obsolescence."

---

[18] Herndon, Astead, *New York Times*, Nov. 7, 2020: "Alexandria Ocasio-Cortez on Biden's Win, House Losses, and What's Next for the Left."

Neither the mainstream Democrats, nor Biden nor Harris, can be considered true friends of progressives and our base – working class people of all colors and genders who need more than merely defeating Trump and Trumpism. That was important, and we blocked with them for that. But we must push for an end to police killings, to homelessness and evictions in the midst of a pandemic. We need an end to the loss of jobs and loved ones to a virulent health crisis that could have been controlled months ago – as it was in other countries. People need an end to spiraling debt, a realistic hope of *having homes*, and a planet to live on past 2030. And we need peace.

Instead of peace there are endless wars and threats of more. Biden's incoming team includes experts in military domination who are eager to continue and intensify the new cold war against China. Their main quibble with Trump on foreign policy was that he was too willing to withdraw troops from Afghanistan, Iraq and Syria. Biden wants the U.S. to "return to the head of the table" globally – in other words, domination as usual. There's no talk of reducing the military budget or stopping the nuclear arms race against Russia and China, or of using those gargantuan funds for domestic programs.

Biden has been ending his speeches with a prayer for "our troops," almost nothing about bringing them home. He voted for the Bush wars in Afghanistan and Iraq. He co-authored the 1994 crime bill that beefed up police forces and intensified mass incarceration of people of color. In 1996 he joined President Bill Clinton to "end welfare as we know it," saying "the culture of welfare must be replaced with the culture of work." (Let's see if he can deliver a massive jobs program now.) In June 2019 he assured a group of Wall Street titans with these words: "No one's standard of living will change, nothing would fundamentally change… I need you very badly. I hope if I win this nomination, I won't let you down. I promise you." A change to the huge gap between rich and poor is not likely without a fight.

Black Voters and the Myth of "Voter Fraud"

On November 6 Biden told African-Americans "I owe you," since their votes put him over the top in Pennsylvania, Michigan, Wisconsin and Georgia. Now he needs to deliver – with an end to police violence, mass incarceration, unemployment, and institutional racism, instead of mere cabinet window dressing. He has made a reasonably good start, but he needs to be held accountable.

Black voters in those states overcame a juggernaut of "voter fraud" allegations designed to suppress Black voters. It was the Republicans' main gambit for winning, and one that has served well for generations, most notably in the 2000 elections. Black leaders in Jacksonville, Florida protested then that their voting rights were denied, and 28,000 ballots in Palm Beach County went uncounted in 2000.[19] Richard J. Hasen, author of *The Voting Wars,* said "The myth that Democratic voter fraud is common, and that it helps Democrats win elections, has become part of the Republican orthodoxy." The late Congressman John Lewis, famous for braving police and their dogs while demonstrating for civil rights and the 1965 Voting Rights Act, said of the "voter fraud" myth that "I thought we'd passed this long ago. But it seems we must fight this over and over."

One celebrating Black voter in Atlanta told TV reporters in November 2020 that she credits Stacey Abrams for the Biden win in Georgia. Abrams "lost" the race for Governor in 2018 to Brian Kemp, who at that time was the Georgia secretary of state. Abrams filed a federal lawsuit claiming that Kemp had impaired citizens' ability to vote, using voter-roll purges and abusing voter-I.D. laws, depriving them of their rights under the First, Fourteenth and Fifteenth Amendments. As founder of Fair Fight Action, Abrams conducted a two-year campaign, traveling to all Georgia counties and registering tens of thousands of people to vote. These numbers made the difference in Georgia on November 3, 2020 – and again on January 5, 2021, in the senatorial runoff.

The battle for democracy is not over. While Trump denounced "vote fraud," the reality has been voter suppression. It's a continuation of Richard Nixon's famous "Southern Strategy" of 1968, Ronald Reagan's promotion of "states' rights" in 1980, George H.W. Bush's Willie Horton campaign ads in 1988, and George W. Bush's manipulation of votes in Ohio and Florida in 2000. In all these cases the goal was to encourage white voters and foster efforts to suppress Black voters. Trump was so incensed it didn't work this time that he mounted a constant barrage of bizarre efforts to change the vote.

The Electoral College and "Winner-Take-All"

Then there's the Electoral College, through which Trump won the presidency in 2016 while losing the popular vote. It's a "winner-take-all" game at state level, no matter how close the vote. And states with smaller populations have a disproportionate number of electors, based on the total of their congressional representatives and senators.

---

[19] Jane Mayer, "The Voter-Fraud Myth," *The New Yorker,* Oct. 29 and Nov. 5, 2012 issue.

The system is a time-worn relic of the Constitutional deal between northern capitalists and southern slavocrats, by which slaves were counted as "three fifths of a person" for purposes of representation in Congress. After the Civil War, Black people were counted as "five fifths," but their votes were suppressed by intimidation and the infamous Black Codes, which denied African-Americans their rights as citizens. The framers of the Constitution never intended for Black people – or women – to vote. It took a century of struggle following passage of the 13th, 14th and 15th Amendments that recognized the rights of the freed slaves after the Civil War. The 1965 Voting Rights Act reinforced those rights and sought to end the Black Codes and massive voter intimidation throughout the former Confederate states.

Long lines at scarce polling places in Black communities, massive purges of voter rolls, plus voter ID requirements and much more show this intimidation continues to the present. Black people in Georgia, Pennsylvania, Michigan and Wisconsin finally beat it back in 2020. But white supremacy continues to reign across the country in myriad ways. The Electoral College reflects the disproportionate number of electors in the South and other states with smaller populations. To solve this injustice we need to abolish the Electoral College, or at a minimum end the "winner-take-all" rule at state level. White southern senators object. According to South Carolina senator Lindsey Graham, "The desire to abolish the Electoral College is driven by the idea Democrats want rural America to go away politically." Rural America is not the problem – racism is. And segregationist Alabama Senator James Allen in 1969 declared "The Electoral College is one of the South's few remaining political safeguards. Let's keep it."

Only a much larger Republican loss in Congress could allow abolition of the Electoral College. So the alternative battle is to end "winner-take-all." The National Popular Vote bill would guarantee the Presidency to the candidate who receives the most popular votes in all 50 states and the District of Columbia. It has become law in 15 states and DC, with a total of 196 electoral votes. It needs an additional 74 electoral votes to go into effect. The bill has passed at least one chamber in nine additional states with 88 more electoral votes. [20]

Georgia voters got a huge victory January 5, 2021, when Rev. Raphael Warnock and Jon Ossoff won two Senate seats, effectively demoting Mitch McConnell to Senate *minority* leader. Georgia had become the epicenter of

---

[20] See www.nationalpopularvote.com.

the fight for democratic rights. Black voters and their white allies, who successfully flipped the state for Biden, mobilized in unprecedented numbers to win. Metro Atlanta DSA issued a statement: "This was a huge victory for grass roots democracy. Organizations led by people like Stacey Abrams fought voter suppression. Others worked hard to activate voters in our Latinx communities. Labor groups like Unite Here put an incredible amount of resources into the race. We donated, canvassed, dropped lit, phone banked, text banked, and voted... And we did it together."

Fighting Against Fascists and *For* Democracy

The January 6 mob assault in Washington was historic. The NY Times said "the assault on the capitol was the first by a large hostile group of invaders since the British sacked the building in 1814." Black Lives Matter activists noted the police response to white gun-toting protesters storming the capitol behind the Confederate flag, while some DC police fraternized and took selfies with them. The mother of Michael Brown, killed by police in Ferguson, Mo., in 2014, told the Washington Post the lack of a police response was stunning: "no shooting, no rubber bullets, no tear gas – nothing like what we have seen."

Trump declared "We will never give up, we will never concede... and that's what this is all about." Rep. Liz Cheney said, "There's no question that the president formed the mob, incited the mob, addressed the mob. He lit the flames." Trump tweeted to the protesters "We love you. You're very special." He later denounced them, backpedaling as pressure mounted against him. Facebook and Twitter took down his words and suspended his accounts. Not quite an impeachment, but it was a hint that Trump's time was over, for a while. Trump was finally impeached for a second time – a historic first. But it fizzled.

In mid-November, following dozens of failed lawsuits to invalidate votes in key states, Trump invited state legislators to the White House, pushing them to refuse to certify the election outcome and then nominate new slates of electors. Prior to Thanksgiving, Trump supporters made death threats to election officials in Arizona, Georgia, Pennsylvania, Michigan and Nevada. In Milwaukee, former sheriff David Clarke declared "We need a chapter of the Proud Boys in Wisconsin because they're the only ones with the courage to get in the face of Black Lives Matter."[21] *(Courage?)*

---

[21] ABC News 12-Milwaukee, November 16, 2020

In Michigan, ten days after the election, 14 men were charged in a plot to kidnap the Governor and take over the capitol building with "200 combatants who would stage a week-long series of televised executions of public officials." Michigan Attorney General Dana Nessel declared: "We are one of the few states that does not ban guns in our state capitol building, and clearly there have been threats made on the lives of our legislators." She added: "In April, we had armed gunmen, some of them the same defendants in this case, that were hovering over state senators with long guns, screaming and yelling at them as they were deliberating ..." The defendants were charged, arraigned, indicted – and released on bond.[22]

Faced with these fascistic threats, labor councils across the country announced plans for a general strike if Trump were to succeed in his attempted coup. These were not the first strike pledges. The People's Strike movement was launched on May Day 2020, by the Jackson Cooperative (of Jackson, Miss.), "*after* we saw working class people launch a wave of labor strike and rent strike actions across the world in response to the severe negligence" in the face of the pandemic. People's Strike builds on the tidal wave of mass marches and rallies led by the Movement for Black Lives in the wake of police murders of George Floyd, Breonna Taylor, and many others.

The millions of unionists and Black Lives Matter marchers vastly outnumber the proto-fascists in Washington and around the country, even though assault weapons and police support favor the fascists.

The Biden team looks less horrifying than Trump's shock troops, of course, but consider this: Richard Stengel, head of Biden's transition team for the U.S. Agency for Global Media, has branded himself "chief propagandist." He is urging the government to use propaganda against its "own population," and says it should "rethink" the First Amendment that guarantees freedom of speech, press and assembly. In 2018 he stated, "Having once been almost a First Amendment absolutist, I have really moved my position on it, because I just think for practical reasons in society, we have to kind of rethink some of those things."[23] Are those "practical reasons in society" the continuous mass protests against police killings? Thousands of people have been jailed for protesting, and have waited months for charges to be dismissed, while thousands more face continued charges for exercising their First Amendment rights.

---

[22] ABC News report by Chuck Goudie, November 18, 2020.

[23] Ben Norton, *TheGrayZone.com*, November 11, 2020.

Regarding people's rights and mass incarceration, neither Biden nor Harris inspire confidence. Biden has specifically rejected calls to defund the police. Harris was a hardline California Attorney General. Her primary challenger Tulsi Gabbard said during the 2020 TV debates: "She put over 1,500 people in jail for marijuana violations and laughed about it when she was asked if she ever smoked marijuana. She blocked evidence that would have freed an innocent man from death row. She kept people in prison beyond their sentences to use them as cheap labor for the state of California, and she fought to keep the cash bail system in place that impacts poor people in the worst kind of way."[24]

At the Chicago Ideas forum in 2011 Harris mocked people who say *"Build more schools, less jails! Put money into education, not prisons!* There's a fundamental problem with that approach," she said. "You still haven't addressed why I have three padlocks on my front door... There should be a broad consensus that there should be serious and severe and swift consequences to crime!"[25] Harris is unlikely to help reverse mass incarceration, or deal with the poverty that breeds crime.

Major financial support for Harris came from Hillary Clinton's biggest backers, who saw Clinton's chances for a 2020 rerun falling flat. Clinton responded to Gabbard's exposé of Harris, and to her anti-war stance, by hinting she was a "Russian agent." Gabbard responded with a defamation suit against Clinton. Harris doesn't come close to repudiating Clinton's bloody record as Secretary of State – fostering fascist coups in Ukraine and Honduras, ordering the murder of President Gaddafi of Libya (and cackling about it), and engineering the disastrous U.S. intervention in Syria.

"Our Task is to Hit the Ground Running!"

Keeanga-Yamahtta Taylor, author of *From #Black Lives Matter to Black Liberation*, told a New York City DSA convention in August 2020: "No matter who wins in November, our task is to hit the ground running" – "ground" as in *streets*. Key demands are defund the police, protest continued police murders, and a full program of people's recovery.

We need to differentiate *our socialism* from Trump's red-baiting. Bernie Sanders says we need a 21st Century Economic Bill of Rights: a job that pays

[24] Caleb Maupin, *Kamala Harris & the Future of America*, New York, 2020, Center for Political Innovation.
[25] www.chicagoideas.com/videos/innovation-evolution-in-our-criminal-justice-system (11:45 – 12:52)

a living wage; quality health care; a complete education; afford-able housing; a clean environment; and a secure retirement. This is an echo of Franklin D. Roosevelt's "economic bill of rights," proposed in his January 1944 State of the Union address. FDR said the "political rights" guaranteed in the Bill of Rights (the first ten amendments to the Constitution) had "proved inadequate to assure us equality in the pursuit of happiness." He said the government should guarantee to all people in the country employment, clothing, and leisure with enough income to support them; farmers' rights to a fair income; freedom from unfair competition and monopolies (for small business owners); housing; medical care; social security; and education for all.

Biden launched his presidency looking like FDR – a flurry of progressive executive orders, and a bold big spending plan. We like the plan. We fought for it. Now we need to make sure it really happens. But we can't expect to get it without a massive popular struggle, just as it took mass mobilizations and strikes led by the left to win FDR's New Deal.

We need a broad popular alliance. The Sunrise Movement says "By joining together – Black, brown, and white – to organize and demand the change we need, we'll make our voices heard in record numbers on the streets and with our votes."

The U.S. Peace Council says "our only way forward is to stay mobilized – demanding justice and accountability against racist killer cops; in defense of migrants rounded up and deported; in solidarity with LGBTQ and disabled people; and against endless wars, sanctions and occupations."

Biden has rejected the call to stop racist militarized policing, to invest in alternatives to policing while cutting police budgets and establishing democratic community control of the police. That just means we have to keep fighting for these things – in the streets, workplaces, and city halls across the country. As Colin Kaepernick wrote recently, instead of police and prisons, "we can create space for budgets to be reinvested directly into communities to address mental health need, homelessness and houselessness, access to education, and job creation as well as community-based methods of accountability. This is a future that centers the needs of the people, a future that will make us safer, healthier, and truly free."

We should mix determination with optimism. There's a dramatic change of mood in the country and rejection of Trump's fascistic measures (with or without Trump). There is a new determination among labor leaders to fight. DSA has forged an alliance with the militant United Electrical Workers union (UE), which says: "The labor movement we need must be a militant movement, built from the bottom up. And it must be based on clear-cut principles: aggressive struggle, rank and file control, political independence, international solidarity and uniting all workers." We can use the alliance with UE to help build fighting unions everywhere. Organizing drives of Amazon, Walmart, Tyson Foods and McDonalds workers, while bolstering militant teachers, nurses, longshore, transport and construction workers, could feel like a CIO revival.

What's most important? Is control of Congress the key? There's a debate brewing about how change happens. All progressives would welcome a congress and president that could deliver Medicare for All, a massive jobs program, a Green New Deal, police reform and all the rest. But if the Civil Rights movement of the 1950s and '60s proved one thing, it's that people marching by the thousands, tens and hundreds of thousands are the main force for change. FDR's New Deal needed intense mass pressure in the streets and factories, which was delivered by huge campaigns organized by the left.

The movement to defund or abolish the police didn't emerge from the 2020 elections. It was the hurricane of people power in the streets that did it. Power sparked by Black Lives Matter multiplied exponentially when working people and youth of all colors and nationalities marched together. The explosive marches focused on defund/abolish. Going forward they will tend to morph into broader struggles on all the issues. It began to happen in the hundreds of strikes, including local wildcats and stoppages, throughout 2020, and in the tenant struggles and rent strikes which have intensified everywhere.

The tenant fight is especially urgent, as millions of people face evictions if federal and state governments fail to intervene. The late December 2020 extension of eviction moratoriums in New York and some other states was a start, but it mainly "kicked the can" a few months down the road. "Tenants won this moratorium," declared DSA's Cea Weaver, a leader of New York's Housing Justice for All coalition. "This moratorium is good news, but it's not a solution to the pandemic housing crisis. We are deeply disappointed that, unlike previous proposals which would have protected tenants for up to a year after the state of emergency ends, the moratorium only lasts until May 1. We also know that any bill that doesn't address back rent is not enough. Albany must still *#CancelRent* along with this eviction moratorium. If they do not, they are potentially condemning hundreds of thousands of New Yorkers to financial ruin as a result of the pandemic."

The coalition mobilized tens of thousands of tenants to push the NY State Assembly to pass the moratorium extension. NYC DSA launched a "Tax the Rich and House the Poor" campaign to get the funds for both housing and green energy in New York. Such a movement needs to be national. There are an estimated 7 to 14 million households at risk of eviction nationally, owing about $20 billion in back rent. There was $1.3 billion in rent relief in the December 2020 federal relief package – not nearly enough to stem a homelessness crisis that threatens to explode from more than 600,000 to many times that number.[26]

Any failure to address the housing crisis will merely intensify the looming real estate credit crisis, which will lead to bank crises that hang over Biden's *debut* like an impending tornado. But it will take a people's tornado to force federal, state and local governments to deal with it.

The strange, ever-rising stock market is not a reflection of a healthy economy. It actually shows that the trillions the Fed pumped into the corporations had nowhere to go in the real economy, so the investor class dumped them onto the stock market. "The market right now is clearly foaming at the mouth," as one market analyst told the New York Times just before Christmas 2020. Another said "We are seeing the kind of craziness that I don't think has been in existence... since the internet bubble" in early 2000. Another said "It's not as obvious a bubble as 20 years ago, but we're close to bubble territory."

Now there's a question for the Biden administration: can it deliver a recovery plan that will mobilize these billions, together with trillions from the military budget and new taxes, to put people back to work converting the country to sustainable energy and guaranteeing health care?

It's an existential question – really "do or die" for Biden. But that's true also for us. A mass people's movement needs to manifest the strength to force real change. As Keeanga-Yamahtta Taylor says, we need to hit the ground running!

And we need to find ways to transform Biden's new beginning into a future that really puts people in charge.

---

[26] See "We Don't Even Count All the Homeless," NY Times editorial, Jan. 29, 2020.

Appendix 1: This article marked the 40th anniversary of the 1975 victory of the Vietnamese national liberation forces.

The power of people's war and global anti-imperialist solidarity

By Dee Knight, April 23, 2015

It took 30 years of hard fighting, but the last weeks were like a blur. First a lightning assault in Vietnam's Central Highlands. Then rapid attacks on the coastal cities of Hue and Danang. Then the People's Liberation Armed Forces converged on Saigon from all sides. The puppet government leaders and hangers-on raced for helicopter liftoffs at the U.S. Embassy, along with Western journalists, embassy staff and camp followers.

The People's Army now had tanks and artillery as well as large-scale regular forces. In every town and village, they met with people's militias and irregular troops who "opened the door" for them. The forces of the Saigon puppet army scattered in the face of their assault.

This April 30 marks the 40th anniversary of Vietnam's 1975 Great Spring Victory. This long, unrelenting war — first against Japan in 1945, then France (supported by the U.S.) from 1945 to 1954, and then directly against U.S. imperialism — defined an era. In 1966, Che Guevara called for "Two, three, many Vietnams!" Vietnam-style struggles emerged in the Portuguese African colonies of Guinea-Bissau, Mozambique and Angola. They achieved victory alongside the Vietnamese. Guerrilla uprisings also surged forth in Central America.

The Vietnamese victory march was planned months in advance. All aspects of the previous 30 years of struggle came into play. There was the Ho Chi Minh trail — a network of roads through jungles and mountains used to funnel a steady supply of weapons, ammunition and food from north to south despite endless U.S. bombing. The tunnels of Cu Chi were strategic underground command and recovery centers. The 1968 Tet Offensive had shown the world what the Vietnamese resistance was capable of.

All these successes were based on the strategy of people's war. "The outstanding characteristic of people's war in our country is that armed struggle and political struggle are very closely coordinated, supporting and stimulating each other," wrote Gen. Vo Nguyen Giap, founder of the People's Liberation Armed Forces (PLAF). "So the slogan 'Mobilize the entire people, arm the entire people and fight on all fronts' has become a most lively and heroic reality."

All efforts by the U.S. to defeat this core strategy — such as the "pacification" and "strategic hamlets" programs — were hopeless. "When a whole people rises up, nothing can be done. No money can beat them," Gen. Giap told the Liberation News Service in 1969. "That's the basis of our strategy and tactics, which the Americans fail to understand.

"All 31 million of our people are valiant fighters," Gen. Giap said, "using a small force to fight a bigger one, defeating a stronger force with a smaller one, combining big, medium-sized and small battles, stepping up big-unit fighting and at the same time carrying out widespread guerrilla warfare, constantly striking the enemy from a strong position and achieving very high combat efficiency, becoming ever stronger and winning ever bigger victories as they fight." (Speech in Hanoi, Dec. 21, 1968)

Mobilization of the entire people meant women, men and children, young and old, countryside and city, north and south. The Saigon puppet administration was penetrated by patriotic spies at all levels. A famous example of the women fighters is the iconic photo of a small peasant woman brandishing her AK-47 as she guided her huge, humbled captive — a downed U.S. bomber pilot — through the forest. Then there is the story of the attentive waitress at a Saigon officers' club frequented by U.S. commanders. After the victory she was publicly honored as a colonel in the PLAF. The entire world came to know Madame Nguyen Thi Binh, who represented the National Liberation Front in the Paris peace talks.

The revolution's leaders were tempered by decades of struggle. For example, Le Duc Tho, famous in the West as Vietnam's lead negotiator in the Paris Peace Talks — who was awarded but rejected the Nobel Peace Prize in 1973 rather than accept it together with war criminal Henry Kissinger — signed the 1975 battle plan for the final spring offensive, on behalf of the Workers Party leadership. Born in 1911, Le Duc Tho had helped found the Indochinese Communist Party in 1930. French colonial authorities imprisoned him from 1930 to 1936 and again from 1939 to 1944. After his release in 1945, he helped lead the Viet Minh, the Vietnamese independence movement against the French, until the Geneva Accords were signed in 1954. From 1948 until 1975, he was a leading organizer for the southern front.

After signing the 1975 battle plan, Le Duc Tho rode to the command center in the Central Highlands, down the Ho Chi Minh Trail by motorcycle, at the age of 64. There he remained, helping to coordinate offensives in three directions until the final march into Saigon.

Global solidarity & international socialist collaboration

Vietnam's victory was global. The Soviet Union, its eastern European allies and the People's Republic of China provided arms, ammunition, food and much more. Anti-war movements in countries across the globe provided very substantial moral support. In the United States, anti-war forces, together with the explosive Black Liberation movement, spawned a large-scale resistance to the war among youth who refused to be part of the war effort. The result was a virtual strike of GIs in the combat zone, as well as rebellions at U.S. military bases across the U.S. and around the world.

The AK-47 rifles used by the Vietnamese People's Liberation Armed Forces were made in Czechoslovakia. The anti-aircraft weapons, as well as trucks, tanks and artillery, were made in the USSR and China. Vietnam was the front line in a global war against U.S. imperialism, and this gigantic solidarity effort was a material factor in Vietnam's victory.

Gen. Giap said in 1968 that "the army and people in North Vietnam have shot down more than 3,200 of the most up-to-date aircraft of the United States, killing or capturing a sizable number of top American pilots, and have sunk or set fire to hundreds of enemy vessels. The so-called air superiority of the U.S. imperialists — the chieftain of imperialism which used to boast of its wealth and weapons and which is notorious for its cruelty — has received a staggering blow at the hands of the Vietnamese people." (Army Day speech, Dec. 21, 1968) This was three years before the PLAF knocked out 30 B-52 Strato-fortresses — a third of the U.S. B-52 fleet — while resisting Washington's last-ditch Christmas bombing of North Vietnam on the eve of the Jan. 27, 1973, peace agreement.

In 1968, Gen. Giap spoke of "all 31 million Vietnamese" fighting U.S. imperialism. Today the population is more than 90 million, making Vietnam the world's 15th most populous country. In 1965, Ho Chi Minh said no matter how many and how much the U.S. might kill and destroy, "We will build up our country many times more beautiful." Since 2000, Vietnam's economic growth rate has been among the highest in the world.

The true legacy of Vietnam, as stated by Gen. Giap, is that "the myth of the invincibility of the United States ... is collapsing irretrievably. No matter how enormous its military and economic potential, it will never succeed in crushing the will of a people fighting for its independence. This is a reality which is now recognized throughout the entire world."

All quotes are from "The Military Art of People's War: Selected Writings of Vo Nguyen Giap," Monthly Review Press, 1970.

Appendix 2:

Sanctuary Movement Supports Surge in GI Resistance

By Dee Knight, January 9, 2009

The current surge in GI resistance has begun to stimulate calls for a sanctuary movement, in which people massively communicate unconditional support for GIs who refuse to fight in the unjust wars in Iraq, Afghanistan and elsewhere. Such a movement is growing in Israel, where dozens of young Israelis have refused to be part of the current genocidal massacre of Palestinians in Gaza.

I spoke with John Lewis, who was a national field organizer of the American Servicemen's Union (ASU) in August 1969, when a gigantic sanctuary struggle took place in Honolulu, Hawaii. The struggle started when Louis "Buffy" Perry entered the Crossroads Church there amid a flurry of publicity on Aug. 6. "I've chosen to begin a lifestyle of non-cooperation, on any level, with the military establishment," Perry told reporters. "I urge all my brothers and sisters to do the same." *(Honolulu Weekly)*

John Lewis and other ASU organizers responded with a march in Honolulu on Aug. 10, led by an alliance of GIs and civilians demanding a "bill of rights" for military personnel. Organizers wanted to form a Hawaii chapter of the ASU. By the end of that day, six GIs went AWOL and sought sanctuary inside the Church of the Crossroads, joining Perry,

The Hawaii People's Coalition for Peace and Justice quickly formed to support the soldiers. Two "sanctuaries" for AWOL soldiers were established: the Church of the Crossroads, and the First Unitarian Church of Honolulu. During the next four weeks, Honolulu, with about 56,000 military personnel stationed on the island, was a hotbed of GI resistance. At least 50 soldiers refused to cooperate in a war they didn't agree with and took refuge in the churches.

"You have to picture the grounds of the Crossroads teeming with people," said Cindy Lance, who stayed at Crossroads Church during the sanctuary struggle. "In the evening there would be maybe a couple hundred support people bringing food and other supplies or just coming to stay for the evening, singing and talking with the GIs."

About dawn on Friday, Sept. 12, military police stormed the two churches and seized some 40 AWOL GIs. The Unitarian Church caretaker remembered waking up with an MP's gun to his head. The raids occurred simultaneously and were over quickly. The soldiers would face court-martial.

"It was a dramatic end to a dramatic demonstration," Unitarian pastor Gene Bridges said of the raid. He explained that the sanctuary idea derives from medieval Christian practice, when a person fleeing authorities could find safe haven inside a church.

Cindy Lance continued to work with Liberated Barracks, an organization spawned by the sanctuary movement that continued to reach out to GIs after the sanctuary raids. "I think the military simply wanted the sanctuary movement to die," Lance said. "They probably thought we would be demoralized after the bust and just fade away. On the contrary, we continued to visit the guys in the brigs and attend their trials."

Many GIs defied the MPs' efforts to arrest them. The cops only caught John Lewis after a dramatic chase across Honolulu by a convoy of vehicles – documented by a BBC-TV news team in Honolulu to cover the sanctuary movement. Lewis ended up in the Fort Dix Stockade in New Jersey, where he participated in a rebellion that destroyed the military prison. Neither he nor anyone else was found guilty of charges connected with the rebellion, since the Brass could not find anyone willing to testify against them.

Other GIs who had participated in the sanctuary decided to leave the country and go to Canada. The life-and-death gravity of the situation changed not only the lives of the GIs, but also the thinking of some anti-war activists. Community members began secretly housing AWOL GIs in their homes.

The Sanctuary movement was integral to the anti-slavery abolitionist movement of the 19th century, known as "the Underground Railroad." Thousands of runaway slaves found freedom and a new life through the heroic support provided to them by churches and individuals who sheltered and guided them, often at extremely high risk to themselves. This legacy is important to the current struggle. Then, as now, those who provided sanctuary were consciously doing everything they could to win immediate freedom for the victims of a criminal government and its institutions arrayed against them.

Today it is likely that a large number of non-white GIs are living a semi-underground AWOL existence, sheltered by their families and other community members. To date, this embryonic form of sanctuary has been largely clandestine. It may be possible to bring it into the open, or at least make it clear to those who remain in hiding that there is widespread public support for them in their communities and in the society at large.

Some worry about the difficulty of providing sanctuary. Cindy Lance commented: "wasn't it difficult for Germans to help Jews escape, or for whites to smuggle slaves to freedom? It's not a question of degree of difficulty, it's a question of doing what's right."

Appendix 3: The following editorial served as the core statement of principles for the campaign for Universal and Unconditional Amnesty

Amnesty and the War:
AMEX editorial March-April 1972

By Dee Knight and Jack Colhoun

The question of amnesty is inextricably connected to that of a total and rapid American withdrawal from Indochina. The fact of an escalated war – escalated vertically into the air with massive bombing and technologically with the use of computerized warfare – is so obvious as to expose the U.S. government's "gradual withdrawal" for the brutal lie that it is.

Many of those in America concerned about amnesty are aware of this. Yet they, like all war resisters, are compelled to discuss amnesty and rescue it from the hands of conservatives, like Republican Senator Robert Taft, Jr., of Ohio, who would use it to prevent justice and disconnect it from the disastrous policies which render it necessary.

Those interested in a just amnesty – one which would be extended to all war resisters with no strings attached – also are aware that the issue can be used to force the government's hand on bringing the war to a true end. We realize that amnesty, if discussed in the context that we were correct to resist forced participation in America's illegal and immoral Indochina debacle, can help an even greater number of Americans understand who are the real criminals of the Indochina era, and where the real causes for the divisions in American society can be found. Discussion of and massive popular pressure for amnesty in this context, we most heartily welcome and support.

But there are a number of things which must be clarified. For instance, the question of "alternative service." Senator Taft and Representative Koch, among others, apparently feel that it is necessary to punish war resisters for having the audacity to see too early that the war was wrong, and worse, to act on our convictions. Thus we must be punished, or if not punished, at least not be "let off scot free" from the obligations which our brothers served. But this strikes us as odd. After the release of the Pentagon Papers and the public introspection which accompanied the Calley trial, we who sacrificed our citizenship or freedom of movement because we knew what was happening and could not be part of it – still we must serve. Must the government have its pound of flesh even as we are forgiven for being right?

Or maybe the motivation for alternative service is more cynical. Maybe the effort is to keep "undesirables" from playing a role in American society, while seeming to have given them the opportunity. It is clear that few exiles would be interested in three years of punishment for doing what we knew was right. And maybe an additional aim of alternative service is to protect the draft, so that it can be used to raise large armies to carry out the same foreign policies which resulted in the Indochina disaster.

Some people argue that after so many have died, their families could not bear to think their sons' lives were sacrificed in vain, and thus amnesty, or at least an unconditional one, is unthinkable. We, like all Americans, feel deeply the loss of those killed on both sides in this horrible war. We agree that all that is possible must be done to allay the grief of the parents and loved ones of those lost. Moreover, these and veterans of Vietnam combat who sustained permanent injuries, must be compensated to the greatest possible extent for their irreplaceable loss.

But the burden of responsibility for these lives must clearly rest with the government leaders who so willingly sacrificed the lives of America's young for no good reason. We who called with our whole being for an end to the killing, must not be blamed for the deaths. We cannot be used as scapegoats. Such can happen when people think that if there was not the level of public opposition that there was, the government would have been able to use a "free hand" to more quickly "win the war."

But what must be understood is that popular opposition was not the main reason America could not "win" in Vietnam. It was and continues to be kind of war that cannot be won, except by destroying completely the land and the people America was supposed to be "protecting." That fact must be the lesson America learns from the Indochina war. And from this it is clear that the responsibility for the lives lost or ruined or damaged on both sides must rest squarely on the U.S. governments which have waged and continue to wage this war.

Some war resisters want very much to share in the job of restoring the government's debt to the people – that is, to help the victims on all sides of this war to mend their lives and get the justice for which all of us have fought for so long. But we need at least the recognition from Americans that we are not criminals, but honest men. This recognition in itself will be a good beginning for the hard work ahead of us.

Some would make us heroes, as others make us cowards. Neither is appropriate. We want neither accolades, apologies, nor scapegoating.

Arrogance, we know, can only interfere in the cause of justice. Most Americans are victims of the disasters of the last ten years. Most are war resisters, in the broad sense of being firmly opposed to the government's war policy. And most are seekers of justice. Thus the only separating which should be done, is that of dividing the peace makers from the war makers, and then fighting for justice.

This brings up the numerous ways that politicians try to separate or categorize war resisters. The effort is to distinguish between those of us who went to jail, those who stayed underground, those who are in stockades or have bad military records which mean a further loss of their civilian rights, and those in exile. Finally, the major distinction is made between all other war resisters, and deserters from the military. We shall answer these one by one.

Those in jail are supposedly more heroic than those who are living underground, or who chose exile. So that paragon of incisive judgment, Julie Nixon Eisenhower is quoted as saying. This argument is at base one which still sees war resisters as criminals. We don't claim to be heroes. Nor do we disparage the way in which others chose to resist. But the whole point of amnesty must be that there is no crime involved in resisting an immoral and illegal war.

There is ample documentation that jail is not a healthy experience. For political prisoners, we are told, life has been made even more miserable by sadistic wardens and guards, in an already inhuman system. Angela Davis' health seriously deteriorated while she was unjustly detained awaiting trial. Prison officials did not even allow her to have the medicines prescribed for her by her doctor. Both of the Berrigan brothers experienced serious problems with their health while in jail. These are just the stories which make headlines because the victims are well-known. We have also learned of the plight of the average prisoner from the writings of George Jackson and Eldridge Cleaver, as well as the rebellions at Attica and elsewhere.

Early in the anti-war movement going to jail was made into a heroic myth. Thoreau was quoted approvingly that the "only place for a man of conscience in America is in jail." But people forget that Thoreau spent only a short time in jail before being bailed out by his friends. This was also the case for many of those who so romantically summoned their followers to jail. Unfortunately however, the less well-known followers often had no bail money, support was not strong for them, and they served and continue to serve long, debilitating jail terms. The anti-war movement outgrew this, but those opposed to amnesty are using it to appear less antiquated, and to discredit and divide war resisters. The anti-amnesty attitude seems to be the "modern" version of the pro-war attitude which is now so out of fashion in America, precisely because of the revelations of the Pentagon Papers and the Calley trial.

One other reason that people may consider going to jail "more heroic" is that in at least one stratum of American society, it is acceptable to honor as heroes those who fight for social justice, after they are crushed or defeated by the forces they seek to change. Thus the image of the loser is held up to the continually defeated for their admiration. But war resisters and all Americans must realize that this time we have not lost, even though the governments and their war planners – who claim to represent us – have lost. The remaining job is to throw out these perpetrators of deceit and defeat.

Then there is the attempt to separate deserters from other war resisters, as if they are even less respectable than those who, while not going to jail, at least did not go into the military. All war resisters know that there is no difference between resisting the war before or after induction. Surely at this juncture in American history, we must all understand that there is no time limit on learning the truth, or waking up to responsibility for our actions.

Draft resisters or pre-induction war resisters, consider the effort to favor them over deserters or other resisters, a cynical attempt at class and race discrimination. It is clear that the war in Indochina has produced nearly an entire generation of draft evaders. The greatest number of evaders never had to *resist* the draft openly. They were able to dodge it successfully primarily because they had options available to them because of their middle-class privileges that were not open to men of the working class and permanent poor because of their class or race origins.

Nearly an entire generation of middle-class sons were exposed to anti-war arguments or were merely opportunistic and decided to evade the draft through college deferments, graduate school deferments when the former expired, the deferred professions such as teaching or perhaps working in defense-oriented industries. ROTC courses carried guaranteed deferments for four years when the other means began to dry up; others used their families' contacts and money to influence draft boards; and finally, the National Guard continued its tradition as a haven for draft evaders. (The *Wall Street Journal* recently published an article on the problems of the National Guard entitled "No Draft, no Dodgers; No Dodgers, No Guard." The Guard five years ago had waiting lists that sometimes ran into the thousands – middle-class sons for the most part, who used their influence to get ahead of other people in their mad rush to get into the Guard and away from the draft.)

Meanwhile, those who could do so used the legal channel of conscientious objector status to get a rubber stamp of approval from the government for their opposition to a war which nobody should have fought. And those of us who couldn't get C.O.'s, or chose for any of many possible reasons not to try, made it successfully into exile. To us, all of these forms of resistance were fine. Each person, according to his situation and his understanding, did what he could to resist.

Amnesty for all of these categories – those of us who have been successful in our resistance largely because of our middle-class origins, and all the others – is meaningful in the context of bringing the war to a definitive end and making Americans understand the causes of the war. But it can only be meaningful if it extends to the men who must traditionally fight America's wars and who always seem to lose in a system where only the rich can win, and only the white are rich.

It could not be more clear that the working class and permanent poor – categories in which Blacks and other third-world peoples are found in great disproportion to their percentage of the population – bore the brunt of the American fighting in Indochina and consequently suffered the largest casualty rates. Many of these men came to understand the fraudulent Madison Avenue techniques used by recruiters to induce them into the military, only when it was too late to use pre-induction methods of resistance which they probably would not have known about anyway.

The men who "volunteered" for service in this war – as has always been the case – were those whose economic situation made them need an alternative. When these men realized how they had been lied to and used, desertion was only one method they have used to resist. And their resistance – both by desertion and inside the military itself – threatens the ability of the government to use deceit and legal pressure to force the disenfranchised Black, poor or working-class youth into fighting an unpopular and illegal war ever again. This is why the President, the Pentagon, and other politicians must oppose amnesty for deserters and resisters still in the military. And this fact clearly exposes the government's insincerity about its "gradual withdrawal" from Indochina, and its lies about "bringing America back together again."

War resisters, whether pre- or post-induction, active or passive, Black or white, want no part of such "amnesties". Unlike the editors of *Newsweek* or

Time, we don't want Americans to forget what caused America's Indochina disaster. Americans must steadfastly and courageously search out the causes of this war, which are clearly the same as the causes of division and poverty in our society, and change them. Otherwise, the manifest destiny of America is to be sucked by the same forces into more Indochinas elsewhere in the world.

The word amnesty means to forget. We are told that the spirit of amnesty will be to forget that there were laws on the books which we violated by resisting war, racism and the draft. Part of this is fine. It will be good if America will forget that we have committed a crime in our resistance, so that those of us who wish or need to be freed from prison, repatriated, or otherwise restored to full citizenship (insofar as that is possible in the present social system), can be. We do not wish to dispute the legal difficulties or terminology under which our citizenship is restored to us.

But we do not wish America to forget the record. Especially, we do not wish voting Americans in this election year to forget the voting records of the politicians who will be trying to sell them various brands of amnesty. For as Senator Kenney admitted at the close of his recent hearings on amnesty, it is really the politicians who are asking the country for amnesty for their past positions on war, and for the laws they made or allowed to exist. And Americans must be rigorous and stern in this matter, if we are to avoid the same disasters at the hands of the same men.

People must beware of the lies and tricks of politicians, on the issue of amnesty as on everything else. One palliative for present ills now widely discussed by politicians from the President on down, is ending the draft. Then, so goes the argument, amnesty would be fine for draft resisters, but still not deserters. Herein the palliative is exposed for what it is: a trick to make people think the military is being demobilized while it is maintained and streamlined – "professionalized" – with America's traditional cannon fodder, the youth of the Black and white working class and poor.

We are opposed both to the draft and a professional army. But what we are most opposed to is a foreign policy which necessitates a huge standing army to further its non-defensive ends. An army needed for truly defensive purposes would have no trouble finding recruits. It is the role of the military in carrying out aggressive war policies which must be opposed by both civilians and those in uniform. And the politicians who try to fool us into allowing their discredited policies to continue, must be exposed.

There has never been a greater lack of credibility in America's so-called "leaders." And no wonder. One politician after another has told us that he is opposed to the war, and then voted the necessary money for its continuation, or merely failed to vote or otherwise use his seat of privilege and influence to stop the killing in Indochina. Can such men be trusted when they offer amnesty to the young who were disenfranchised when their lives were placed on the line in one way or another by this war?

Amnesty: a Yard Stick

Amnesty can be used as a yard stick of the honesty of these men. If a politician says he is for amnesty, the people must ask him if this would include deserters. If his answer here is no, or if he waffles on this, he is not to be trusted. Ask him what strings are attached. If he talks about some kind of "alternative service," perhaps the people should suggest some alternative service for him instead of his job as "the people's advocate."

But this cannot be enough. Most American politicians, clearly, do not merit the support of the American people. If they have been part of the government's lying, genocidal war effort, how can they be supported? In some places, it will be possible or practical to try and replace them. In others it will be futile. Some people remain disenfranchised by the vagaries of gerrymandering, the rigging of nominations, by press monopolies, poll tax, literacy tests and all the rest.

In such cases people may wish to circulate petitions calling for universal, unconditional amnesty. In others, especially near stockades or federal prisons, people may wish to hold rallies calling for the release of jailed war resisters and all political prisoners. GI's and other workers, as they strike for better working conditions, higher pay and for control of the products of their labors, may wish to include amnesty for war resisters and other political prisoners in their demands. Veterans of Indochina combat, as they fight for jobs and re-entry to the society which used them in the war, have already begun the demand for universal, unconditional amnesty which includes GI's in resistance and those given less than honorable discharges.

All these things we support. We encourage individuals and groups to request written statements from the President and other politicians as to their position on the war and amnesty – ask for the politicians' voting record on all bills related to the war; and we urge groups and individuals to make written, public statements calling for universal, unconditional amnesty for all war resisters and other political prisoners.

We warn people to beware of legislative or other administrative action on amnesty. Especially beware of those who counsel for a quiet, non-public discussion at this level. This is where the sell-out would take place – a fact which becomes clear when we consider who controls the Senate and House committees where amnesty legislation would have to be considered: the most conservative, anti-democratic elements in American politics. Further, we warn against the use of amnesty simply to "rationalize" the legal status of conscientious objectors to war. Amnesty must be broad, with the intent of granting legal immunity to all who resisted this illegal war effort. And the only way this will come about is with massive and sophisticated public debate and popular pressure.

Above all, we encourage those Americans who would fight for amnesty on our behalf, that they never fail to link it to the demand for a rapid and total withdrawal of all American intervention in the affairs of the peoples of Indochina, or any place else in the world.

Appendix 4: Book Review –

Refusing to commit war crimes – and testifying

By Dee Knight, Feb. 16, 2008

*The Deserter's Tale: The Story of an Ordinary Soldier
Who Walked Away from the War in Iraq,* by Joshua Key

*Road From Ar Ramadi: The Private Rebellion of
Staff Sergeant Camilo Mejia,* By Camilo Mejia

(Also reviewed: *Letters from Fort Lewis Brig: A Matter of Conscience,* by Sgt. Kevin Benderman; *Mission Rejected: U.S. Soldiers Who Say No to Iraq,* by Peter Laufer; *Dissent: Voices of Conscience – Government Insiders Speak Out Against the War in Iraq,* by Colonel (Ret.) Ann Wright and Susan Dixon)

"TRAINED TO KILL – KILL WE WILL!" That's what U.S. Army recruits must shout while marching to the mess hall for a meal. That's all it took for Private Jeremy Hintzman to know he had to get out. He was the first U.S. war resister from the Iraq war to seek refugee status in Canada.

It took a little longer for Private Joshua Key, but he was not "gung ho." If you fail to show sufficient enthusiasm, you're "smoked." "They made me do push-ups, duck walks, crawl around on my hands and knees, and stand at attention while every man in my platoon hollered that I was a 'useless asshole' and a 'stupid shit'," said Private Key in The Deserter's Tale.

"One day, all 300 of us lined up on the bayonet range, each facing a life-size dummy that we were told to imagine was a Muslim man. As we stabbed the dummies with our bayonets, one of our commanders stood at a podium and shouted into the microphone: 'Kill! Kill! Kill the sand n----rs!' We were made to shout out [the same thing]. While we shouted and stabbed, drill sergeants walked among us to make sure we were all shouting. It seemed the full effect of the lesson would be lost on us unless we shouted out the words of hate as we mutilated our enemies."

That was basic training. Key remembers advanced training with the 43rd Combat Engineer Company. His "officers' repeat-ed warnings: 'If you feel threatened, kill first and ask questions later.' I had army chants buzzing through my head, like 'Take a playground, Fill it full of kids. Drop on some napalm, And barbecue some ribs.'"

The real thing was yet to come. In Iraq, Key's first duty assignment was to set off explosives to blast open doors of Iraqi people's homes, join a six-person assault team storming in to terrorize everyone inside, and take prisoner any male over five feet tall. "We put our knees on their backs, pulled their hands behind them, and faster than you can bat an eye we zipcuffed them. Zipcuffs are plastic cuffs that lock on tight. They must have bit something fierce into those men's skin... The Iraqi brothers were taken away to an American detention facility for interrogation... I never saw one of them return to the neighborhoods we patrolled regularly."

Later Key had to pull guard duty in front of a hospital in Ramadi, for weeks on end. A little girl who lived near the hospital would run up to the fence he was guarding and "call out the only English words she knew: 'Mister, food!' " Key said "she was about seven years old. She had dark eyes, shoulder-length brown hair, and – even for a young child – seemed impossibly skinny. She usually wore her school uniform – a white shirt with a blue skirt and a pair of sandals... She seemed fearless, full of energy, and not the least bit frightened by my M-249. She acted as if she didn't even know that she lived in a war zone, and she ran to the fence the same way my own children might have approached a sand box, piping out, 'Mister, food!' "

Key would tell the girl to go away, but when she insisted, he would give her his MRE rations (the nearly inedible "Meals Ready to Eat"). She would run away home. "Her visits were the best part of my days at the hospital, and she was the only person in Iraq... whose smile I enjoyed.... I wasn't the only soldier in our squad who gave rations to the girl..."

Several weeks into his guard duty at the hospital in Ramadi, Key said "I was back at my post in front of the hospital. I saw the girl run out of her house, across the street, and toward the fence that stood between us. I reached for an MRE, looked up to see her about ten feet away, heard the sound of semiautomatic gunfire, and saw her head blow up like a mushroom...

"My own people were the only ones with guns in the area, and it was the sound of my own people's guns that I had heard blazing before the little sister was stopped in her tracks. I saw her mother fly out the door and run across the street. She and someone else in the family bent over the body. I could feel them all staring at me, and I could say nothing to them and do nothing other than hang my head in shame while the family took the child away."

"Her death haunts me to this day," Key said. "I am trying to learn to live with it."

The bulk of Private Key's duty in Iraq was "busting into and ransacking homes… Before my time was up in Iraq, I took part in 200 raids… We never found weapons or indications of terrorism. I never found a thing that seemed to justify the terror we inflicted every time we blasted through the front door of a civilian home, broke everything in sight, punched and zipcuffed the men, and sent them away…"

American terrorists

"It struck me," Key said, "that we, the American soldiers, were the terrorists. We were terrorizing Iraqis. Intimidating them. Beating them. Destroying their homes. Probably raping them. The ones we didn't kill had all the reasons in the world to become terrorists themselves. Given what we were doing to them, who could blame them for wanting to kill us, and all Americans? A sick realization lodged like a cancer in my gut. It grew and festered, and troubled me more with every passing day. We, the Americans, had become the terrorists in Iraq."

Joshua Key was a dirt-poor 19-year-old from Guthrie, Oklahoma, trying to put food on the table for his young wife, Brandi, and their two infant children by delivering pizza. He was lured in by an Army recruiter promising a decent wage, a stateside job, and money for training so he could realize his dream of becoming a welder.

His experiences in Iraq "got me thinking," he said. "How would I react if foreigners invaded the United States and did just a tenth of the things that we had done to the Iraqi people? I would be right up there with the rebels and insurgents, using every bit of my cleverness to blow up the occupiers. I would dig a hole in my hometown in Oklahoma and rig mines in the trees and set them to blow up when the enemy passed below. I would lob all the mortars and rocket-propelled grenades I could buy. No doubt about it. If somebody blasted into my home and terrorized my family, I would become a force to be reckoned with…"

Staff Sergeant Camilo Mejia's experiences were essentially identical to those of Private Joshua Key. Except he was a squad leader. When he and his squad were ordered to blast into an Iraqi home, he was responsible to make sure it was done properly. And to deal with his men afterward – including when the orders they carried out subjected them to unnecessary danger. Mejia said he and his men were ordered to "draw the enemy out" in "fierce firefights and roadside bomb attacks, most of which could easily have been avoided." Tensions and resentment mounted, and "I heard rumors that soldiers in our unit were plotting [the commander's] assassination."

Both Mejia and Key had sufficient direct experience of being ordered to commit war crimes in Iraq that they had enough. As soon as they were allowed out of Iraq on leave, they decided not to come back. Mejia chose to refuse publicly and apply for conscientious objector status. He was rejected, and was sentenced to a year in military prison and a bad conduct discharge.

Key just left. He rejoined his wife and their three small children, and went underground. They lived desperately on the run for over a year. Key used his skills in welding and mechanics to work, running the risk of being arrested or turned in, driving without a valid license, living in constant fear of being stopped for a minor traffic violation and then busted for desertion. Finally, after "googling" the Internet with "deserter needs help," he got in touch with the War Resisters Support Campaign in Toronto. *(See Appendix 7.)*

"Sucking up the courage to drive to the border of my own country was the hardest thing I had ever done," he said. "It would have been easier in some ways to go back to war and serve my time. It would have caused me a lot less stress to sit in a jail cell. But I didn't want to participate in an unjust war, and I didn't believe it was right that I should become a prisoner in my own country for refusing to act like a criminal in Iraq. I felt that the only right choice was to move forward, and I did so with my wife and my children beside me."

Camilo Mejia found support for his refusal here in the U.S. – first with the Citizen Soldier support organization and its legal director Todd Ensign, and later with the pacifist Peace Abbey, which gave him sanctuary until he turned himself in to fight for his right to be recognized as a conscientious objector.

Despite losing his case before the military kangaroo court, and serving nine months in military prison, Camilo Mejia came out of prison fighting, and has traveled around the country speaking and organizing. He is now the chairperson of Iraq Veterans Against the War (IVAW), and deeply involved in building for the Winter Soldier Hearings to be held in mid-March [2008] in Washington, DC.

A growing number of others have followed Mejia's lead. In December 2004, Navy Petty Officer Pablo Paredes, from the Bronx, refused to board ship in San Diego and sail to the Persian Gulf. He didn't want be "part of a ship that's taking 3,000 Marines over there, knowing a hundred or more of them won't come back." He said he "never imagined, in a million years, we would go to war with somebody who had done nothing to us."

After his May 2005 court martial, Pablo Paredes was sentenced to three months hard labor while confined to base, and then discharged. He then became a counselor for the GI Rights Hotline. That year the Hotline reported an estimated 32,000 individual callers, about 30 percent of whom were asking for help with being AWOL. Tens of thousands of GIs have gone AWOL since the U.S. invasion of Iraq in March 2003. About 11,000 have deserted, according to Pentagon figures.

African-American GIs are not a visible part of the resistance community, which does not, of course mean Black GIs are not resisting. The Pentagon figures make it obvious that the vast majority of resisters are living underground in the U.S. And of course, Canada is far less often perceived as an option for a young Black man, despite the fact that racism is less intense and strident in Canada than it is in the U.S.

Lieutenant Ehren Watada, who in January 2006 became the first officer to refuse to serve in Iraq, told the Veterans For Peace Convention in August of that year, "I speak with you about a radical idea. It is one born from the very concept of the American soldier (or service member). It became instrumental in ending the Vietnam war... The idea is this: that to stop an illegal and unjust war, the soldiers can choose to stop fighting it." But, he said "those wearing the uniform must know beyond any shadow of a doubt that by refusing immoral and illegal orders, they will be supported by the people not with mere words but by action... To support the troops who resist, you must make your voices heard."

In November 2005, Congressman John Murtha, a Pennsylvania Democrat and veteran of 37 years in the Marine Corps, switched from supporting to opposing the U.S. war in Iraq. Why? "The future of our military is at risk," he told Congress. "Our military and their families are stretched thin. Many say the Army is broken. Some of our troops are on their third deployment. Recruitment is down... Personnel costs are skyrocketing... Choices will have to be made..."

To answer the recruitment problem, Bush and Cheney chose to use mercenaries instead of instituting the draft. It's an understandable choice. They feared a massive rebellion of youth across the country, as well as an even more intense rebellion within the ranks of the military. But it has been an expensive choice – one the current generation of workers is paying for, as will our children, since they have had to borrow massive sums from the banks to pay for their rent-a-soldiers, who earn about $1,000 a day, and answer to no one. No wonder there is less and less money for people's needs, or to help people reclaim their homes in New Orleans.

The GIs who have refused also made their choices. And they have begun to change history.

IVAW has found enormous interest and support among both veterans and active-duty GIs to testify at the Winter Soldier Hearings about their experiences in Iraq. And the organization has become a potent force in organizing GIs both here in the U.S. and in Iraq, to oppose the illegal and racist orders they receive as standard operating procedure. Most recently, IVAW has built vibrant chapters among active duty soldiers at Fort Lewis, Washington, and Fort Drum, New York – the major deployment points for combat duty in Iraq. They also have chapters at other bases, including Fort Bragg, North Carolina – the "home of the Airborne" – Camp Pendleton Marine Base near San Diego, and Fort Hood in Texas.

IVAW has the strong support of Veterans For Peace, the Vietnam-generation group that has thousands of members nationally. The two generations of veterans have forged a strong bond, based on their common experience of having been ordered to commit war crimes in senseless wars of aggression. They also share the experience of finding strong support in the general population when they tell the truth they were forced to live: that the government had sent them to war with lies and terror. The truth they tell is hard to refute.

Appendix 5:
Calls for unconditional amnesty for military resisters to current U.S. wars in Iraq, Afghanistan and Pakistan

By Dee Knight, April 9, 2010, Berkeley, Calif.

In the first action of its type during the current U.S. wars in Iraq, Afghanistan and Pakistan, the Berkeley, Calif., City Council on March 9 passed a resolution entitled, "Universal and Unconditional Amnesty for Iraq, Afghanistan, and Pakistan War Military Resisters and Veterans Who Acted In Opposition to the War for Matters of Conscience," according to a report from Courage to Resist.

"Amnesty" means that any charges or remaining punishment are officially "forgotten." "Unconditional" means no strings attached. "Universal" means it would apply to all convictions or pending charges related to resistance to or refusal to serve in the current U.S. wars, as well as going absent without leave.

This amnesty would include all veterans with less than honorable discharges for such resistance. The call adds that such veterans should have their discharges automatically upgraded to honorable, and that they should be entitled to all benefits.

Bob Meola, Berkeley Peace and Justice Commissioner who wrote the original draft of the resolution, stated, "I hope this resolution will serve as a model and inspire cities and towns across the United States to pass similar resolutions and ignite a movement which will result in Universal and Unconditional Amnesty for Iraq, Afghanistan, and Pakistan war resisters and veterans.

"The troops who have had the courage to resist have been traumatized enough. They have followed their consciences and deserve healing and support and appreciation from people everywhere. The GI Resistance movement is growing. Its members are heroes and sheroes and should be treated as such when they are welcomed back into civilian society."

The new resolution deepens the city's anti-war commit-ment, which in 2007 made Berkeley a "sanctuary city" for military resisters and draft registration resisters.

First demanded during war on Vietnam

To end punishment of U.S. resisters to the Vietnam war, the newsletter of U.S. war resisters in Canada at that time, AMEX/Canada, in 1973 was first to formulate the demand for universal unconditional amnesty. The demand became the focus of a broad campaign based on an alliance of exiled war resisters, anti-war veterans and active-duty GIs, with strong support from pacifist, civil liberties and religious groups.

The campaign featured bold defiance of government efforts to punish resisters, who would "surface" at anti-war conferences, political conventions and congressional hearings — most often unannounced — demonstrating widespread support for resistance and amnesty.

This campaign induced President Jimmy Carter to grant unconditional amnesty to resisters following the U.S. War in Vietnam, in January 1977. Carter felt the pressure after one exiled resister, Fritz Efaw, surfaced at the 1976 National Democratic Convention as part of the "Democrats Abroad" delegation, and was nominated for vice president by Gold Star mother Louise Ransom (whose son was killed in Vietnam combat). Disabled Vietnam veteran Ron Kovic, author of "Born on the Fourth of July," seconded the nomination, and stunned the delegates into total silence followed by a standing ovation.

Amnesty for all!

In the wake of last month's gigantic demonstration in Washington, D.C., by immigrants and their supporters calling for full and complete legalization for all people in this country without official documentation, the new call for amnesty for war resisters should simply extend to include both groups.

The same is true for sanctuary — a type of solidarity that has been extended for decades to both groups by churches, unions, cities and individuals. The concept of sanctuary actually emerged in the Middle Ages, when churches often had parallel power with civil authorities. A person or group could seek protection in a church from oppressive authorities and thus avoid capture and punishment.

Today, just as in the past, the fight for amnesty and sanctuary is a battle for the right to resist unjust governmental power. And it is a way for progressive people to exercise their own power and force an end to militarism and racism.

For regular updates on the GI resistance, see www.CourageToResist.org.

Appendix 6: Pentagon downplays GI suicides

By Dee Knight, New York, Feb. 12, 2009

The Pentagon reported in January that "Suicides among soldiers rose for the fourth straight year, exceeding the rate for civilians for the first time in decades." (Associated Press, Jan. 29) A graph showed the increase—from about 80 GI suicides in 2003 to almost 150 in 2008.[27]

Despite this admission, the Pentagon was downplaying the suicide story. The problem is much bigger, according to a new book by Iraq war correspondent Aaron Glantz: "The War Comes Home: Washington's Battle Against America's Veterans." A November 2007 CBS News investigation, says Glantz, found that 120 veterans kill themselves every week – over 6,000 per year. Glantz cites internal Veterans Administration documents validating these figures: "There are about 18 suicides per day among America's 25 million veterans" of all wars, said the VA's chief of mental health, Ira Katz.

Glantz says the Pentagon's report, covering only active-duty GIs, is an underestimate, "in part because they only include confirmed suicides. Many suicides are simply called accidents." Garrett Reppenhagen, a former Army sniper in Iraq, told Glantz a woman in his unit "died when she shot herself in the chest with her M-16. The Army said it was an accident, but you can't accidentally shoot yourself in the chest with an M-16... ."

Post-Traumatic Stress Disorder afflicts nearly half a million Iraq and Afghanistan war vets. It is a prime cause of suicide, accidental death, and death at the hands of police — which some veterans provoke as a form of suicide.

Glantz tells of Sgt. James Dean, who was shot by Maryland state troopers on Christmas night in 2006 while sitting alone in his father's farmhouse. Dean had returned home from 18 months in Afghanistan with what the VA diagnosed as PTSD: "The patient states he feels very nervous, has a hard time sleeping, feels nauseous in the a.m., and loses his temper a lot, 'real bad.'" The evaluation mentions that Sgt. Dean "was nearby an explosion that

---

[27] According to a June 2021 report from the "Costs of War Research Series" by Brown University's Watson Institute for International and Public Affairs, an estimated 30,177 active duty personnel and veterans of the post 9/11 wars have died by suicide, significantly more than the 7,057 service members killed in post-9/11 war operations.

destroyed a Humvee with four GIs killed in front of his eyes. ... The patient is tired of feeling bad."

Dean "barricaded himself inside his farmhouse. ... He called his sister and told her he 'just couldn't do it anymore' and fired a gunshot. Jamie's sister called the emergency services hotline and the police showed up in force. ... Just past midnight ... a police sharpshooter shot Jamie Dean dead."

It might have cost less, and saved a life, to mobilize a psychological crisis team, but that's not the police way, or the Army way.

According to Glantz, by August 2008 "the Pentagon listed more than 78,000 service members as wounded, injured or ill; 324,000 Iraq and Afghanistan veterans had already visited a VA facility to receive health care for their injuries, and close to 300,000 (more than 30 percent of eligible veterans) had filed for disability.

"Physical brain damage is perhaps the most common injury; the RAND Corporation estimates that more than 320,000 veterans have experienced traumatic brain injury (TBI) while deployed in Iraq or Afghanistan. Many observers call TBI the 'signature injury' of the Iraq War because it happens so often after a soldier is hit with a gunshot or a blast from a roadside bomb."

Rather than accept responsibility for the suffering of its veterans, the military machine punishes them. Take the case of Specialist Shaun Manuel, who was ordered to do a second tour in Iraq on the heels of losing his infant son.

Glantz tells the story: "Manuel never filed paperwork to medically excuse himself from the deployment. Instead, he withdrew and buried himself in alcohol. He estimates he drank three fifths of liquor a day. At one point, his wife had to call the police during a domestic disturbance. In response, the Army threw him in a local county jail and kicked him out of the military with a bad-conduct discharge, which will deny him medical benefits he might have been able to use to get his life back together again."

The parents of Corporal Jeffrey Lucey of Belchertown, Mass., tell of filing a lawsuit alleging "wrongful death, medical malpractice, pain and suffering, and other damages" caused by the VA's "negligence, carelessness and lack of skill" in treating their son, who hanged himself in his parents' home in June 2004.

The Marine Corps had told Lucey's parents it was "normal for veterans to need some time to adjust after their return from the war zone." Lucey's father said the Marine Corps told them, "Whatever you do, don't force them or pressure them to do something they don't feel comfortable doing."

Maybe the whole military establishment and their civilian commanders should memorize that warning. Perhaps members of the House and Senate should be required to say it over and over again before passing legislation authorizing the president to use troops overseas.

Appendix 7: Changing Faces of Military Resistance

Chelsea Manning became the most famous GI whistle blower *ever* by exposing U.S. war crimes in Iraq in 2010, as Pfc Bradley Manning. Convicted by court martial in 2013, and sentenced to 35 years, she was continuously brutalized in military prisons. Faced with a massive global campaign, Obama commuted her sentence in January 2017. She

has again braved prison for refusing to testify against Julian Assange.

Army Reserve **Captain Brittany DeBarros** rebelled against her 14-day activation in July 2018, with "daily posts… about the horror being carried out by our war machine for profit." Speaking at the Poor People's Campaign rally in Washington DC, as a combat veteran, woman, Latina, white, Black, and queer, she said as a person "existing at the intersection of these identities, I carry a grave conviction in my core that there can be no true economic, racial, gender liberation without addressing the militarism that is strangling the morality and empathy out of our society."

Cadet Spenser Rapone posted a picture of himself in his West Point uniform holding a sign that said, "Communism will win" tucked under his hat, raising a clenched left fist; and another picture with a Che Guevara T-shirt under his uniform, captioned "In case there was any lingering doubt, *hasta la victoria siempre*".

He also had another with the words #VeteransForKaepernick — referring to the first football player to kneel during the national anthem at a football game to protest racism. The Army accepted his resignation in June 2018.

Rapone has also posted a picture of himself holding up the Communist Manifesto, with his Army dress uniform hanging in the closet in the background. Rapone and Iraq vet Mike Prysner launched the "Eyes Left" podcast to advocate rebellion in the U.S. armed forces.

André Shepherd is a U.S. military resister who applied for asylum in Germany in November 2008 – the first Iraq War veteran to do so. His first claim was denied in 2011, so he appealed to the European Court of Justice, which sent the case back to Germany to determine "whether US soldiers were committing war crimes in Iraq and whether Shepherd risked being involved in such crimes if he went." Shepherd plans to appeal the court's verdict against him. He has a permit to remain in Germany because his wife is German.

Meanwhile in **Canada**, support for U.S. war resisters was strong enough that many made their homes there. They received support from trade unions, churches and prominent individuals, but not from the government.

RESOLUTION

Recognizing the duty of the Federal Government
to create a Green New Deal.

Whereas the October 2018 report entitled "Special Report on Global Warming of 1.5°C" by the Inter-governmental Panel on Climate Change and the November 2018 Fourth National Climate Assessment report found that—

(1)   human activity is the dominant cause of observed climate change over the past century;

(2)   a changing climate is causing sea levels to rise and an increase in wildfires, severe storms, droughts, and other extreme weather events that threaten human life, healthy communities, and critical infrastructure;

(3)   global warming at or above 2 degrees Celsius beyond preindustrialized levels will cause—

(A)   mass migration from the regions most affected by climate change;

(B)   more than $500,000,000,000 in lost annual economic output in the United States by the year 2100;

(C)   wildfires that, by 2050, will annually burn at least twice as much forest area in the western United States than was typically burned by wildfires in the years preceding 2019;

(D)   a loss of more than 99 percent of all coral reefs on Earth;

(E)   more than 350,000,000 more people to be exposed globally to deadly heat stress by 2050; and

(F)   a risk of damage to $1,000,000,000,000 of public infra-structure and coastal real estate in the United States; and

(4)   global temperatures must be kept below 1.5 degrees Celsius above preindustrialized levels to avoid the most severe impacts of a changing climate, which will require—

(A)   global reductions in greenhouse gas emissions from human sources of 40 to 60 percent from 2010 levels by 2030; and

(B)   net-zero global emissions by 2050;

Whereas, because the United States has historically been responsible for a disproportionate amount of green-house gas emissions, having emitted 20 percent of global greenhouse gas emissions through 2014, and has a high technological capacity, the United States must take a leading role in reducing emissions through economic transformation;

Whereas the United States is currently experiencing several related crises, with—

(1) life expectancy declining while basic needs, such as clean air, clean water, healthy food, and adequate health care, housing, transportation, and education, are inaccessible to a significant portion of the United States population;

(2) a 4-decade trend of wage stagnation, deindustrialization, and antilabor policies that has led to—

(A) hourly wages overall stagnating since the 1970s despite increased worker productivity;

(B) the third-worst level of socioeconomic mobility in the developed world before the Great Recession;

(C) the erosion of the earning and bargaining power of workers in the United States; and

(D) inadequate resources for public sector workers to confront the challenges of climate change at local, State and Federal levels; and

(3) the greatest income inequality since the 1920s, with—

(A) the top 1 percent of earners accruing 91 percent of gains in the first few years of economic recovery after the Great Recession;

(B) a large racial wealth divide amounting to a difference of 20 times more wealth between the average white family and the average Black family; and

(C) a gender earnings gap that results in women earning approximately 80 percent as much as men, at the median;

Whereas climate change, pollution, and environmental destruction have exacerbated systemic racial, regional, social, environmental, and economic injustices (referred to in this preamble as "systemic injustices") by disproportionately affecting indigenous peoples, communities of color, migrant communities, deindustrialized communities, depopulated rural communities, the poor, low-income workers, women, the elderly, the unhoused, people with disabilities, and youth (referred to in this preamble as "frontline and vulnerable communities");

Whereas, climate change constitutes a direct threat to the national security of the United States—

(1) by impacting the economic, environmental, and social stability of countries and communities around the world; and

(2) by acting as a threat multiplier;

Whereas the Federal government-led mobilizations during World War II and the New Deal created the greatest middle class that the United States has ever seen, but many members of frontline and vulnerable communities were excluded from many of the economic and societal benefits of those mobilizations; and

Whereas the House of Representatives recognizes that a new national, social, industrial and economic mobilization on a scale not seen since World War II and the New Deal era is a historic opportunity—

    (1) to create millions of good, high-wage jobs in the United States;

    (2) to provide unprecedented levels of prosperity and economic security for all people of the United States; and

    (3) to counteract systemic injustices: Now therefore be it

    Resolved, That it is the sense of the House of Representatives that—

    (1) it is the duty of the Federal government to create a Green New Deal—

        a.   to achieve net-zero greenhouse gas emissions through a fair and just transition for all communities and workers;

        b.   to create millions of good, high-wage jobs and ensure prosperity and economic security for all people of the United States;

        c.   to invest in the infrastructure and industry of the United States to sustainably meet the challenges of the 21st century;

        d.   to secure for all people of the United States for generations to come—

            i. clean air and water;

            ii. climate and community resiliency;

            iii. healthy food;

            iv. access to nature; and

            v. a sustainable environment; and

        e.   to promote justice and equity by stopping current, preventing future, and repairing historic oppression of indigenous peoples, communities of color, migrant communities, deindustrialized communities, depopulated rural communities, the poor, low-income workers, women, the elderly, the unhoused, people with disabilities, and youth (referred to in this resolution as "frontline and vulnerable communities");

    (2) the goals described in subparagraphs (a) through (e) of

paragraph (1) (referred to in this resolution as the "Green New Deal goals") should be accomplished through a 10-year national mobilization (referred to in this resolution as the "Green New Deal mobilization") that will require the following goals and projects—

a.   building resiliency against climate change-related disasters, such as extreme weather, including by leveraging funding and providing investments for community-defined projects and strategies;

b.   repairing and upgrading the infra-structure in the United States, including—

    i. by eliminating pollution and green-house gas emissions as much as technologically feasible;

    ii. by guaranteeing universal access to clean water;

    iii. by reducing the risks posed by climate impacts;

    iv. by ensuring that any infrastructure bill considered by Congress addresses climate change;

c.   meeting 100 percent of the power demand in the United States through clean, renewable, and zero-emission energy sources, including—

    i. by dramatically expanding and upgrading renewable power sources; and

    ii. by deploying new capacity;

d.   building or upgrading to energy-efficient, distributed, and "smart" power grids, and ensuring affordable access to electricity;

e.   upgrading all existing buildings in the United States and building new buildings to achieve maximum energy efficiency, water efficiency, safety, affordability, comfort, and durability, including through electrification;

f.   spurring massive growth in clean manufacturing in the United States and removing pollution and greenhouse gas emissions from manufacturing and industry as much as is technologically feasible, including by expanding renewable energy manufacturing and investing in existing manufacturing and industry;

g.   working collaboratively with farmers and ranchers in the United States to remove pollution and greenhouse gas emissions from the agricultural sector as much as is technologically feasible, including—

    i. by supporting family farming;

    ii. by investing in sustainable farming and land use practices that increase soil health; and

    iii. by building a more sustainable food system that ensures universal access to healthy food;

h.   overhauling transportation systems in the United States to remove pollution and green-house gas emissions from the transportation sector as much as is technologically feasible, including through investment in—

    i. zero-emission vehicle infrastructure and manufacturing;

    ii. clean, affordable, and accessible public transit; and

    iii. high-speed rail;

i.   mitigating and managing the long-term adverse health, economic and other effects of pollution and climate change, including by providing funding for community-defined projects and strategies;

j.   removing greenhouse gases from the atmosphere and reducing pollution by restoring natural ecosystems through proven low-tech solutions that increase soil carbon storage, such as land preservation and afforestation;

k.   restoring and protecting threatened, endangered and fragile ecosystems through locally appropriate and science-based projects that enhance biodiversity and support climate resiliency;

l.   cleaning up existing hazardous waste and abandoned sites, ensuring economic development and sustainability on those sites;

m.   identifying other emission and pollution sources and creating solutions to remove them; and

n.   promoting the international exchange of technology, expertise, products, funding, and services, with the aim of making the United States the international leader on climate action, and to help other countries achieve a Green New Deal;

(3) a Green New Deal must be developed through transparent and inclusive consultation, collaboration, and partnership

with frontline and vulnerable communities, labor unions, worker cooperatives, civil society groups, academia, and businesses, and

(4) to achieve the Green New Deal goals and mobilization, a Green New Deal will require the following goals and projects—

    a.   providing and leveraging, in a way that ensures the public receives appropriate ownership stakes and returns on investment, adequate capital (including through community grants, public banks, and other public financing), technical expertise, supporting policies, and other forms of assistance to communities, organizations, Federal, State and local government agencies, and businesses working on the Green New Deal mobilization;

    b.   ensuring that the Federal government takes into account the complete environmental and social costs and impacts of emissions through—

        i. existing laws;

        ii. new policies and programs; and

        iii. ensuring the frontline and vulnerable communities shall not be adversely affected;

    c.   providing resources, training and high-quality education, including higher education, to all people of the United States, with a focus on frontline and vulnerable communities, so that all people of the United States may be full and equal participants in the Green New Deal mobilization;

    d.   making public investments in the research and development of new clean and renewable energy technologies and industries;

    e.   directing investments to spur economic development, deepen and diversify industry and business in local and regional economies, and build wealth and community ownership, while prioritizing high-quality job creation and economic, social and environmental benefits in frontline and vulnerable communities, and deindustrialized com-munities, that may otherwise struggle with the transition away from greenhouse gas intensive industries;

    f.   ensuring the use of democratic and participatory

processes that are inclusive and led by frontline and vulnerable communities and workers to plan, implement, and administer the Green New Deal mobilization at the local level;

g.   ensuring that the Green New Deal mobilization creates high-quality union jobs that pay prevailing wages, hires local workers, offers training and advancement opportunities, and guarantees wage and benefit parity for workers affected by the transition;

h.   guaranteeing a job with a family-sustaining wage, adequate family and medical leave, paid vacations, and retirement security to all people of the United States;

i.   strengthening and protecting the right of all workers to organize, unionize, and collectively bargain free of coercion, intimidation, and harassment;

j.   strengthening and enforcing labor, workplace health and safety, antidiscrimination, and wage and hour standards across all employers, industries and sectors;

k.   enacting and enforcing trade rules, procurement standards, and border adjustments with strong labor and environmental protections—

i.   to stop the transfer of jobs and pollution overseas;
ii. to grow domestic manufacturing in the United States;

l.   ensuring that public lands, waters and oceans are protected and that eminent domain is not abused;

m.   obtaining the free, prior, and informed consent of indigenous peoples for all decisions that affect indigenous peoples and their traditional territories, honoring all treaties and agreements with indigenous peoples, and protecting and enforcing the sovereignty and land rights of indigenous peoples;

n.   ensuring a commercial environment where every businessperson is free from unfair competition and domination by domestic or inter-national monopolies; and

o.   providing all people of the United States with—

i.   high-quality healthcare;
ii. affordable, safe and adequate housing;
iii. economic security; and
iv. clean water, clean air, healthy and affordable food, and access to nature.

178

Appendix 9:
Oppose Escalating U.S./NATO Cold War Against China

June 21, 2021

All fair-minded people need to take a fresh look at the escalating U.S. cold war against China.

Source: Global Network Against Weapons & Nuclear Power in Space

According to President Biden and most of the U.S. Congress, China has become a serious threat that must be countered in every way, and in every corner of the globe. The U.S.-led cold war against China has escalated quickly and dramatically. President Biden has tried to harness the G7 and NATO to isolate China, and Congress is fast-tracking bills to counter China's Belt and Road Initiative and punish China for alleged human rights violations.

This escalation is not new. Barack Obama launched the U.S. "pivot to Asia." Now the seas around China bristle with U.S. aircraft carriers and nuclear submarines, while missiles and super-bombers are pointed at China from Japan, Korea, Thailand, the Philippines, Indonesia and Australia, with tens of thousands of troops.

The U.S. recently forged the "Quadrilateral Security Dialog," or Quad Alliance, with Japan, India and Australia, to further challenge China. But it's not enough. Biden wants *all* U.S. allies to join sides against China.

There's a problem with this strategy. According to a *NY Times* report of June 16, "Not all countries in NATO or the Group of 7 share Mr. Biden's zeal to isolate China." Germany, France, Italy, Greece, and several other European countries have major economic ties with China. French President Emmanuel Macron told *Politico* "NATO is an organization that concerns the North Atlantic. China has little to do with the North Atlantic." NATO now stretches to the Russian border, and even reaches the Chinese border with Afghanistan. In 2011 it took part in crushing Libya and murdering President Muammar Gadhafi.

The people of Europe don't want war. A survey by the European Council on Foreign Affairs in January found that most Europeans want to remain neutral. Only 22% would want to take the U.S. side in a war on China, and just 23% in a war on Russia. The Alliance of Democracies Foundation (ADF), in Europe, conducted a poll of 50,000 people in 53 countries between February and April 2021, and found that *more people around the world (44%) see the United States as a threat to democracy in their countries than China (38%) or Russia (28%).* That makes it hard for the U.S. to justify war in the name of democracy. In another poll of 124,000 people ADF conducted in 2020, countries where large majorities saw the United States as a danger to democracy included China, but also Germany, Austria, Denmark, Ireland, France, Greece, Belgium, Sweden and Canada.

ADF also studied the disparity between those who believe in democracy and those who think they live in one. The chart on the next page shows *73% of Chinese think their country is democratic, while just 49% in the U.S. believe their country is democratic.*

Another report – from Harvard University's Ash Center for Democratic Governance and Innovation – finds over 90% of the Chinese people like their government, and "rate it as more capable and effective than ever before. Interestingly, more marginalized groups in poorer, inland regions are actually comparatively more likely to report increases in satisfaction." It says Chinese people's attitudes "appear to respond to real changes in their material well-being." Elevating 800 million people out of extreme poverty probably helped.

This contrasts with people's attitudes in the United States, which are polarized politically, racially, and economically. Public trust in government is in crisis. This could be a reason for politicians to whip up a cold war fever –

and an urgent reason for socialists to take the danger seriously. We need to highlight very real human rights concerns at home, where police killings, homelessness and mass incarceration are at pandemic proportions.

BBOViz / **Democratic deficits**

**Many who believe in democracy
don't feel they live in one**

2020	% My country is democratic		% Democracy is important
Australia		58	71
Brazil	51		83
Canada		65	78
Chile	42		73
China		73	84
France	52		77
Germany		67	85
Hong Kong	37		64
India		71	82
Iran	28	50	
Italy	54		83
Japan	46	60	
Mexico	52		77
Poland	38		86
Russia	39		66
Saudi Arabia	53	63	
South Korea		75	85
U.K.	58		75
U.S.	49		73
Venezuela	24		74
	0 25 50 75 100		

In the U.S. Congress, there has been bi-partisan support for the Innovation and Competition Act, which demonizes China's economic successes across the globe. Charges fly that China favors its companies, both private and state-owned, in China and elsewhere, through subsidies and special financing, while subjecting western trade partners to forced technology transfer, theft of intellectual property, and more. The proposed response is for the U.S. government to do much the same. In Europe Biden announced a "build back better" western version of global infrastructure development, but when and whether it will happen is unclear.

Bernie Sanders wrote in *Foreign Affairs* in June 2021 that "a fast-growing consensus is emerging in Washington that views the U.S.-Chinese relationship as a zero-sum economic and military struggle..." Bernie said "the rush to confront China has a very recent precedent: the global 'war on terror.'

In the wake of the 9/11 attacks, the [U.S.] political establishment quickly concluded that antiterrorism had to become the overriding focus of U.S. foreign policy. Almost two decades and $6 trillion later, it's become clear that national unity was exploited to launch a series of endless wars that proved enormously costly in human, economic, and strategic terms and that gave rise to xenophobia and bigotry in U.S. politics – the brunt of it borne by American Muslim and Arab communities. It is no surprise that today, in a climate of relentless fearmongering about China, the country is experiencing an increase in anti-Asian hate crimes."

Accusations on Human Rights

The incessant accusations of Chinese government abuse of human rights in Hong Kong and Xinjiang have recently been the subject of critical examination. CodePink reports that "since 2014 the U.S. government has pumped a staggering $30 million into opposition movements within China through the National Endowment for Democracy (NED). Much of that funding went to groups which organized the recent Hong Kong protests, as well as to the East Turkestan separatist movement in Xinjiang. *(Source: the NED's online grants database.)* Allen Weinstein, a NED founder, told the Washington Post "A lot of what we do… was done covertly… by the CIA."

Hong Kong native Julie Tang, a retired judge of the San Francisco Superior Court, said recently the 2019 Hong Kong riots began as a political protest against the extradition of a confessed murderer, but were supported by "a shadow power" – the NED – in an attempt to destabilize China through destruction and violence. Rioters killed a 70-year-old man by hitting him with a brick, and doused another with gasoline and burned him. They broke into the parliament building – much like the January 6, 2021 fascist riot in DC.

Tang observes that Hong Kong ranks in the top three on the Fraser Human Freedoms Index, while the USA is in 17th place. She quotes Hong Kong journalist Nury Vittachi that "Hong Kong's civil unrest was the most reported news story of 2019 – yet every salient detail presented was incorrect… The city's freedoms had not been removed… Police killed no one… Agents from a global superpower were intimately involved, but it wasn't China."[28] Rioters branded the Hong Kong police as "public enemy #1," despite remarkable police restraint – in contrast to police behavior across the USA in 2020.

---

[28] Nury Vittachi, *The Other Side of the Story: A Secret War in Hong Kong,* 2020, ASIN

The 2019 riots in Hong Kong failed, Judge Tang says. "Now there is peace in Hong Kong, but there is a proposed U.S. law to devote $300 million to anti-China propaganda."

Independent Canadian reporter Daniel Dumbrill reports that the East Turkestan Islamic Movement (ETIM), which has claimed responsibility for attacks in Xinjiang and elsewhere in China, has been identified as a terrorist organization by the governments of China, Kazakhstan, Pakistan, Turkey and the United States. The U.S. government removed ETIM from its list of terrorist organizations in October 2020, and has provided funds to it through NED. Following explosive incidents of terrorist violence by ETIM, the Chinese government responded with repression. But it also instituted a large-scale job training program, as part of its national anti-poverty crusade. On a personal visit to Xinjiang, Dumbrill found that a very small minority of Uyghurs were repressed, and a large portion benefited from job training.

Responding to official U.S. charges of forced labor and genocide, Zhun Xu, an associate professor of economics at John Jay College in New York, says "if [China] has engaged in forced assimilation and eventual erasure of a vulnerable ethnic and religious minority group," there should be a decrease in the Uyghur population and increase in the Han. But Xinjiang's Uyghur population increased by 24.9 percent from 2010 to 2018, while the Han population in Xinjiang grew by only 2.2 percent. [29]

Right-wing religious extremist Adrian Zenz, who states he is "led by God" on a "mission against China," is the main source for U.S. government and media criticism of Xinjiang conditions. He is also funded by The Jamestown Foundation, an arch-conservative defense policy think tank in Washington, DC, which was co-founded by William Casey, Reagan's CIA director. Other important sources are the World Uyghur Congress, the International Uyghur Human Rights and Democracy Foundation, and the Uyghur American Association – all of which receive substantial NED funding. [30]

Other sources, according to Ajit Singh, include the Australian Strategic Policy Institute (ASPI) and Washington, DC-based Center for Strategic and International Studies (CSIS) – both militaristic think tanks funded by US and western governments and weapons manufacturers. ASPI and CSIS

[29] Cited by Reese Ehrlich, in *The Progressive,* February 2019, from Zhun Xu's upcoming book, *Sanctions as War.*

[30] Ajit Singh, *thegrayzone.com/2020/03/26,* "'Forced labor' stories on -China Brought to You by the US Gov, NATO, Arms Industry"

successfully spearheaded a campaign against "forced labor" in Xinjiang, stimulating moves in Congress to ban U.S. imports from Xinjiang.

Professor Kenneth Hammond of New Mexico State University recently explained the two main aspects of Chinese government policy towards ethnic and religious minorities: first, to *preserve and respect* their language and culture, and second, *inclusion and opportunity* through education, health care and job training. Improved health care programs in Xinjiang have contributed to life expectancy increasing there from 31 years in 1949 to 72 currently.[31] In 1949 there were 54 medical centers in Xinjiang; now there are more than 7,300 health care facilities and more than 1,600 hospitals. Literacy has increased from 10% to over 90% in the same period.[32] Average income has increased more than 10% since 2017.[33]

Tens of millions of Chinese people practice the Islamic faith. Of China's 55 officially recognized minority peoples, ten are Sunni Muslim.[34] There are more Islamic mosques in China than the United States. Uyghurs are the second-largest group, after the Hui. A large proportion of Uyghurs practice a moderate form of Islam called Sufism,[35] which promotes an ascetic lifestyle and shuns material wants. Sufism is incompatible with radical Islamic fundamentalism and Wahhabism, extremist beliefs which have been associated with terrorism in recent decades. The overwhelming majority of Uyghurs are not militant or extremist in outlook.

Over the past generation Washington and the CIA have provided consistent support to Uyghur separatist organizations, and terrorist groups such as the Turkistan Islamic Party (TIP), led by Abdul Haq al-Turkistani. The TIP, originally calling itself East Turkestan Islamic Movement, received direct CIA funding and sponsorship.[36] Abdul Haq has served on Al Qaeda's executive leadership council. He calls for jihad (holy war) against China to

---

[31] D.V. Buyarov, A.A. Kireev, A.V. Druzyaka, "Demographic Situation in Xinjiang-Uigur Autonomous Area in the Last Quarter of the Twentieth Century", *Global Media Journal*, 24 June 2016

[32] Xin Gao, "Education in Xinjiang," *Borgen Magazine*, 4 December 2017

[33] Mark O'Neill, "A growing economy is key to China's control of Xinjiang," *The Article*, 1 March 2020

[34] Ethnic minorities in China, *Wikipedia.org*

[35] Shane Quinn, "Beijing's Decades-long Policies in Xinjiang," *Orinoco Tribune*, 13 March 2021

[36] Luiz Alberto Moniz Bandeira, *The Second Cold War: Geopolitics and the Strategic Dimensions of the USA*, Springer, 2017, p. 68

attain the TIP's separatist goals. Prior to the summer 2008 Olympic Games in China, Abdul Haq ordered the TIP to unleash terrorist attacks against a number of cities in mainland China. Almost all of them were foiled. Following China's clampdown in Xinjiang starting in 2017, no terrorist acts have since taken place in the province.

Reports of first-hand delegations to Xinjiang from countries and organizations including Egypt, Pakistan, Afghanistan, India, Indonesia, Russia, Kazakhstan, Kyrgyzstan, Thailand, Malaysia, the Organization of Islamic Cooperation, and even the World Bank, have testified that neither genocide nor slavery accurately describe the realities of Xinjiang.[37] At two separate convenings of the UN Human Rights Council in 2019 and 2020, letters condemning Chinese conduct in Xinjiang were outvoted, 22-50 and 27-46 – essentially the U.S. and its allies *vs* non-aligned countries. Many of those standing in support of Chinese policy in Xinjiang are Muslim-majority nations and/or nations that have waged campaigns against extremism on their own soil, including Iraq, Palestine, Pakistan, and Nigeria.

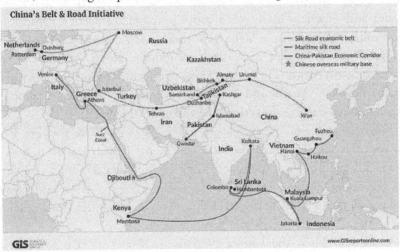

Why has the United States backed separatism and terror in Xinjiang? CodePink points to "a concerted attempt by the U.S. in recent decades to balkanize China by delegitimizing, or creating disruption, in North Korea, Hong Kong, Taiwan, the South China Sea, Tibet and Xinjiang. Dismembering China has been a long-term goal of the U.S. government since 1949. Now Xinjiang is the linchpin of China's Belt and Road Initiative

---

[37] "Xinjiang: A Report and Resource Compilation," QiaoCollective.com, 21 September 2020

(BRI), and a rich resource, producing 85% of China's cotton and 25% of its oil.

Xingjiang's largest cities, Urumqi and Kashgar, are main hubs on the BRI's "Silk Road economic belt," with rail links from Kashgar through Pakistan to the Indian Ocean, and from Urumqi through Central Asia to Teheran, Istanbul, Moscow, and western Europe.

No wonder the U.S. wants to stop it! It's the biggest infrastructure project in human history. It's linking China across Eurasia and parts of Africa – 65 countries and more than 4 billion people. But the BRI is *economic, not military.* That may be its main threat. Take the case of Africa.

Comparing U.S. and Chinese Activity in Africa

There is a stark contrast between U.S. and Chinese political, economic, and security sector activity in Africa. The U.S. Africa Command maintains military presence in fifty African countries, and has staged *coups d'etat* at least seven times in the past decade – Libya in 2011, Mali in 2012, 2020 and 2021, Egypt in 2013 and Burkina Faso in 2015. U.S. trade and finance policies and practices in recent decades have amounted to a neo-colonial regime often referred to as a "debt trap" that has left most African countries impoverished. Until the mid-1980s America's closest African ally was apartheid South Africa. The United States and its European allies, principally Britain, France, Portugal and Belgium, have fiercely resisted or sabotaged African decolonization efforts since the end of World War 2.

Kenya's President Uhuru Kenyatta said in 2018 that "We are very keen as a country, and I believe also as a continent, to partner strongly with China." Liberia's Economy Minister Augustus Flomo said "China is a very, very important partner for our development strategy." Both leaders were speaking on the occasion of the 2018 Forum on China-Africa Cooperation, which was attended by nearly all Africa's leaders.

In May 2021 at the United Nations in New York, China's Foreign Minister Wang Yi announced, together with African countries and the African Union (AU), the launch of an Initiative on Partnership for Africa's Development. The emphasis is "to provide greater impetus to Africa's independent and sustainable development." It focuses on response to COVID-19 and post-COVID reconstruction, trade and investment, environmental protection, debt relief, agriculture, agro-industry, sustainable development, infrastructure, energy and transport, scientific and technical cooperation, digitalization and industrialization." It calls for more vaccines for Africa, and to help build African capacity to manufacture vaccines by waiving intellectual property protections for COVID-19 vaccines. As of April 5, 2021, China had donated vaccines to more than 80 countries and exported vaccines to more than 40 countries. As of March 2021, China had shared 48% of domestically-manufactured vaccines with other countries through donations and exports.[38]

The statement said Africa is a stage for international cooperation, not an arena for big-power competition: "this Initiative adheres to multilateralism and is open to all countries and international organizations in the world ... under the principle of 'African ownership, equality and openness'."

Chinese foreign direct investment (FDI) in Africa surged from US $75 million in 2003 to US $2.7 billion in 2019. Chinese FDI flows to Africa have exceeded those from the U.S. since 2014, which have been declining since 2010. China-Africa bilateral trade has been steadily increasing for the past 16 years. The value of China-Africa trade in 2019 was $192 billion. The largest exporter to China from Africa in 2019 was Angola, followed by South Africa and the Republic of Congo. Nigeria bought the most Chinese goods in 2019, followed by South Africa and Egypt.

---

[38] China's vaccine map: Aid to more countries with 1st EU GMP certificate, CGTN, 5 April 2021

While China's trade with Africa has surged in the past decade, U.S.-Africa trade has plummeted, from a 2008 high $113.5 billion in imports from Africa to $23.7 billion in 2020. U.S. exports declined from $28.39 billion in 2008 to $22.15 billion in 2020 – total trade was about $46 billion,[39] slightly more than one fifth of China's trade with Africa.

Chinese global foreign aid expenditures increased steadily from 2003 to 2015, growing from US $631 million in 2003 to US $3 billion in 2015. Between 2013 and 2018, 45 percent of China's foreign aid went to Africa. For the USA, total global "economic and military assistance" totaled about $50 billion in 2017, of which about $15 billion was military – roughly 30 per-cent – according to USAID's *Foreign Aid Explorer* website. Total U.S. economic assistance to the top eleven African recipient countries in 2017 was approximately $7.5 billion; military assistance was about $1.5 billion, according to the same source. (Based in Germany, Africom's budget may not be included in U.S. military assistance figures for Africa.)

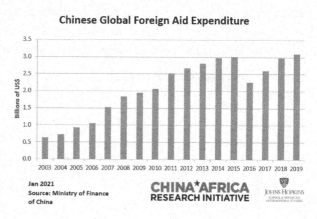

Chinese Global Foreign Aid Expenditure

Jan 2021
Source: Ministry of Finance of China

CHINA★AFRICA
RESEARCH INITIATIVE

JOHNS HOPKINS

Africa's debt to U.S. banks and multi-lateral lending institutions – the World Bank and the International Monetary Fund (IMF) – is another story. "Structural Adjustment Programs," or SAPs, have been the primary mode of the U.S.-Africa financial relationship. These programs forced African countries to pay off debts with *increased* debt in exchange for austerity and privatization measures. African nations have paid over four times the amount of their original debt to World Bank and IMF lenders since 1980.[40] These debt payments bleed Africa of billions of dollars each year.

[39] U.S. Census: www.census.gov/foreign-trade/balance/c7910.html
[40] "Is American 'Aid' Assistance or Theft? The Case of Africa," in *American Exceptionalism and American Innocence,* by Roberto Sirvent and Danny Haiphong, Skyhorse, New York, 2019.

By contrast, China's economic cooperation includes *concessional loans*, at below commercial interest rates, grants, and interest-free loans. China has *cancelled debt* to Africa's least developed countries.

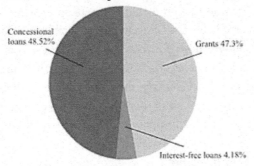

Concessional loans 48.52%

Grants 47.3%

Interest-free loans 4.18%

China's Foreign Aid in Three Categories, 1913-1918

While China's commercial interest in Africa is clear – it needs mineral resources and oil – it provides significant value in return. Infrastructure projects like sea ports, airports, railroads, highways and digital connectivity grab headlines. Sharing China's own experience in poverty reduction, reversing desertification, and green energy are also important. So are industrial and agricultural assistance programs.

"Chinese are outmaneuvering the U.S. in select countries in Africa," General Stephen Townsend, commander of AFRICOM, told Associated Press late in April. He said the Chinese are "looking for a place where they can rearm and repair warships..."

This has been disputed by Deborah Bräutigam, director of the China Africa Research Initiative at Johns Hopkins School of Advanced International Studies, who wrote in the Washington Post that "many of the things our politicians believe about Chinese engagement are not actually true." She added that China's economic engagements in Africa are not of a predatory nature, but are "very much in line with the economic interests of these African states, providing jobs to locals and improving public infrastructure."

Brautigam's book *Will Africa Feed China?* debunks myths of Chinese "land grabbing" in Africa, according to Amadou Sy of the Brookings Institution's Africa Growth Initiative.[41] Brautigam wrote that "interest in China's role as an overseas agricultural investor in Africa has generated hundreds of newspaper articles and editorials, sensational statements and

[41] Amadou Sy, "What Do We Know About the Chinese Land Grab in Africa?" Brookings Institution, November 5, 2015.

robust myths – but surprisingly little investigative reporting." She found that out of over 6 million hectares of alleged Chinese land acquisitions, only 252,901 hectares had actually been acquired. In 2021 the UN's Food and Agriculture Organization found that Chinese enterprises working in Africa are making concerted efforts to engage in responsible agriculture.

China's officially stated principles for development cooperation[42] include:

- *Respecting each other as equals*: "When cooperating with other countries for development, no country should interfere in their efforts to find a development path suited to their own national conditions, interfere in their internal affairs, impose its own will on them, attach political strings, or pursue political self-interest."

- *Focusing on development and improving people's lives*, it increases investment in poverty alleviation, disaster relief, education, health care, agriculture, employment, environmental protection, and climate change response, and actively participates in emergency humanitarian relief operations.

- *Providing the means for independent development*, China shares its experience and technologies, and trains local talent and technicians, to empower them to tap their own potential for diversified, independent and sustainable development.

- *Conducting effective cooperation in diverse forms*, including: complete projects, goods and materials, technical cooperation, cooperation in human resources development, South-South Cooperation Assistance Fund (SSCAF), medical teams, outbound volunteers, emergency humanitarian aid, and debt relief.

China is committed to a multi-lateral approach. By the end of 2019, China had launched 82 projects under the South-South Cooperation Assistance Fund framework in cooperation with 14 international organizations, including the United Nations Development Programme (UNDP), World Food Programme (WFP), World Health Organization (WHO), United Nations Children's Fund (UNICEF), United Nations Population Fund (UNFPA), United Nations High Commissioner for Refugees (UNHCR), International Organization for Migration (IOM), and International Committee of the Red Cross (ICRC). These projects cover agricultural development and food security, poverty reduction, health care for

---

[42] *China's International Development Cooperation in the New Era*, State Council White Paper, 10 January 2021, http://english.www.gov.cn/

women and children, response to public health emergencies, education and training, post-disaster reconstruction, migrant and refugee protection, and aid for trade. The two largest program areas are agricultural development and food security (37.89%), and poverty reduction (37.71%)

China has also set up funds in the World Trade Organization and the World Customs Organization for building trade capacity and helping developing economies, and particularly the least developed countries, to integrate into the multilateral trading system.

China is not looking for war with the United States. And "China has no intention of building a parallel international economic system, competing with the one led by the U.S. China has been a key beneficiary of globalization in the past several decades and has a great stake in continuing that open and integrated international system." The Belt & Road Initiative – of which much of China's engagement with Africa is a part – could "not only significantly increase living standards for 64% of the world population... but also become a new segment of the global supply chain, contributing to world economic growth."[43]

Such a development should be seen as positive, not as a threat.

The real threat today is war over Taiwan. During the Trump years the U.S. broke from recognizing the "one China policy" agreed to by Nixon in 1972, sending cabinet level officials to meet with Taiwanese leaders, and openly engaging in military cooperation. This continues under Biden, backed up with U.S. nuclear-armed war ships, just like 1958, when a crisis threatened to escalate into nuclear holocaust. We need to stop this war before it starts.

"What would happen to the world," Judge Julie Tang asks, "if the United States and China were to go to war? The price of war would be calamitous. We need to aim for peace, not war. China is not our enemy."

---

[43] Yiping Huang, "Understanding China's Belt & Road Initiative: Motivation, Framework and Assessment," *China Economic Review,* Vol. 40, Sept. 2016, pp. 314-321

About the author:

Since this book is really the story of my life and beliefs, it is itself my best identifier. Here's a bit more: I have lived in New York City since 1974, except 1987 to 1990, when I lived and worked with the Sandinistas in Nicaragua. I lived in Toronto, Canada, from August 1968 until August 1974. From 1965 to '68 I studied, first at University of San Francisco and then at San Francisco State College. I left SF State in January 1968, and went to Canada in August of that year. I was born in Cottonwood, Idaho, and grew up in Pendleton, Oregon. I graduated from high school in 1964, with a scholarship to study at the University of Oregon in Eugene, but instead I went to a Jesuit seminary in Los Gatos, California, where I lasted just four months — didn't much like silent penitence or the prospect of lifelong celibacy!

While in Canada I completed a BA in English at York University. I returned to the USA in 1974, first to work as a full-time organizer for the National Council for Universal Unconditional Amnesty. I then got "an honest job" as a typesetter, then moved to desktop publishing. I took this skill to Nicaragua, where I worked as a volunteer consultant for the Sandinista newspaper *Barricada,* and later for several other progressive publishers there. In 1991 I began a five-year consultancy with the UN Development Programme (UNDP) in New York, first as editor of a staff newsletter on computer technology, and later as specialist in electronic document management and groupware. At that time I also completed a Masters in Public Administration at New York University. After leaving UNDP I completed graduate credits in education to be certified as a teacher of high school English and Social Studies, and worked in South Bronx alternative high schools for several years. I have also worked as a writer of both political journalism and technical documentation.

As detailed in this book, I have been a dedicated activist for social change ever since 1968.

Index